Psalms
for
People Under Pressure

Psalms
for
People Under Pressure

BY

JONATHAN AITKEN

continuum
LONDON • NEW YORK

Continuum
The Tower Building, 11 York Road, London SE1 7NX
15 East 26th Street, New York, NY 10010

www.continuumbooks.com

First published 2004

British Library Cataloguing-in-Publication Data
A catalogue record for this book is available from the British Library.

ISBN 0-8264-7275-3

Typeset in Postscript Sabon by Tony Lansbury, Tonbridge, Kent.
Printed and bound in Great Britain by The Cromwell Press, Trowbridge,
Wiltshire.

To Elizabeth

CONTENTS

PART III

UNDERSTANDING GOD WHEN UNDER PRESSURE

The translations used for all the psalms in this book are taken from the New International Version (NIV) of the Bible.

PREFACE

If you have started to read this book, the chances are that you have had some experience of being under pressure.

So welcome to the club! What you may not know is that the club is extremely old. Three thousand years ago its poets composed their own spiritual guide for coping with the stressful emotions and situations in their lives. This is the Book of Psalms. It is a collection of songs of experience which, in beautiful Hebrew poetry, distil the wisdom of the ages on the pressures faced by the ancient people of Israel during the first millennium B.C.

Although the outward forms of pressure have changed between that era and the 21st century, the inner sources of pressure remain remarkably similar. There are many aspects of the human condition that transcend time. The Israelites often felt over-whelmed by familiar negative forces such as pain, tension, depression, loneliness, insecurity and an inability to cope with life's problems. They were troubled by special vicissitudes such as hostility from enemies, betrayal by friends, torment from unjust accusers and alienation from family. Like people down the ages they suffered from yearnings of love, pangs of guilt and the agonies of physical and mental ill-health. Their personal malaises included restlessness of the soul, envy of the successful, emptiness of the spirit and anxiety of the mind in many forms. In times of such painful emotions, and at the times when their hearts were full of joy, the people of Israel communicated with God through the psalms.

Even in our own less Godly era, many of these ancient experiences will strike a chord with contemporary people feeling under pressure. If so, they may find the psalms to be a treasure trove of answers and antidotes relevant to some of the most stressful situations in modern times. This was my discovery and one I wanted to share with others by writing this book. For during a period of maximum pressure in my own life I found the psalms to be spiritual gold seams of wisdom, comfort and guidance.

I stumbled on the riches of the psalms in a prison cell at a moment of acute fear on the worst day of my life.

On 8 June 1999 I was sentenced to 18 months imprisonment on charges of perjury arising out of a lie I had told on oath in a civil libel case. After being driven away from the Central Criminal Court through jeering crowds in a 'sweat box' or prison van, the next few hours were a non-stop nightmare of grim experiences. They were part of my 'Induction' – the name for the initiation and registration procedures all new arrivals in British prisons have to go through. At HMP Belmarsh, one of London's largest and toughest jails, Induction is a gruelling routine. Its rituals include strip searching; mug-shot photography; fingerprinting; confiscation of personal items of property; issue of ill-fitting prison uniform; psychiatric interviews; medical investigations; and cell allocations. All these processes are shared amidst a great deal of noise and shouting with your fellow occupants of 'the cage'. This is an appropriately animalistic and iron-barred enclosure in which all newly sentenced prisoners arriving from the courts are held for their first few hours of incarceration.

Business was brisk in the Belmarsh cage on the evening of 8 June. About 35 men were being inducted into the prison in visible states of distress that ranged from the despondent to the desperate. In the last category was a young black prisoner who kept charging into the bars of the cage like a frenzied bull until he split his head open and had to be restrained in a straitjacket, streaming blood over the prison officers. Another excitable young man tried to escape, which was an enterprise doomed to failure in the heart of Britain's highest security prison. Elsewhere in the cage several members of a robbery gang were fighting among themselves, kicking and punching one of their number for getting the script of his evidence wrong in a way which had allegedly brought all the gangsters guilty verdicts. In various corners several heavily tattooed characters were sitting with heads buried in their hands. One or two of them were weeping. I was feeling pretty low myself, but at least I had already come to terms with the inevitable consequences of my decision to plead guilty. It also helped that I felt my sentence was fair and in line with expectations.

Eventually my hours in the cage ended when a prison officer handed me a slip of paper and said: 'Aitken, you're going to Beirut.' I had no idea what he meant but I followed him off to House Block 3 which I later discovered is nicknamed after the capital of war torn Lebanon because it houses so many toolmen (gunmen) in its cells.

My hope was to get my head down and sleep at the end of an exhausting and testing day. No such luck. My arrival at Belmarsh had been well reported on the evening TV news bulletins. So within minutes of getting to Beirut I was the target of a cat-calling exercise known as 'doing a quizzy'. This consisted of bellowing questions and answers, quiz-style, from one House Block to another across the exercise yards. Over the next few weeks I heard many quizzies on the theme of what the partici-pants would like to do to various unpopular prisoners or prison officers. It was just a nightly opportunity for hotheads to let off hot air, much of it fuelled by drug-taking. However, on my first evening as a prisoner I had no experience of Belmarsh's sounds and furies signifying nothing. So my heart froze as I realised that the raucous dialogue of the 8 June quizzy was entirely directed at me. 'Where's (expletive deleted) Aitken?' 'What are we going to do to (expletive deleted) Aitken?' 'How do we (expletive deleted) well give Aitken a good (expletive deleted) up his (expletive delet-ed)?' were among the politer questions in the chant. The gist of the answers were that tomorrow morning they would (expletive deleted) well give this or that type of (expletive deleted) beating to this or that part of my (expletive deleted) body.

Read in cold print long after the event, the over-the-top obscenities of that quizzy look absurd. But at the time they scared me. The morning newspapers had not been backward in suggesting that a Cabinet Minister who becomes a convict might expect to have one or two difficult moments during his sentence.

However, nothing had prepared me for the viciousness, the venom and the violence of that quizzy. So I was terrified. I felt utterly helpless and totally vulnerable. The pressures of fear inflamed my already raw nerve-ends in agonising pain. But what on earth could I do about it?

For some months before the date of my sentencing I had been travelling on a spiritual journey. It was largely the pressures of adversity that had set me off on this voyage of exploration. Those pressures had included defeat, disgrace, divorce, bankruptcy and jail – a royal flush of crises by anyone's standards. Yet pressure can be a making as well as a breaking experience. For after several false starts, stumbles, doubts and backslidings, my voyage of exploration gradually evolved into a committed quest for a right relationship with God. On the evening of the Belmarsh quizzy it therefore seemed natural to turn to his divine power with a *cri de coeur* for help since in the frightened loneliness of my cell no earthly power was capable of offering me protection. So I knelt down on the concrete floor and tried to say a prayer.

Because I was so petrified by the shouts of menace around me at first I found it impossible to say even the simplest words of supplication. Then I remembered that just before going off to the Old Bailey to be sentenced a friend had put into my pocket a calendar style booklet entitled 'Praying the Psalms'. When I was searched on arrival at Belmarsh it was confiscated for drug examination by sniffer dogs. But it was later returned to me with the explanation that it qualified under paragraph 71(c) of the Prison Rules as a 'religious book'. So I turned up the page for 8 June. It recommended reading Psalm 130. As I studied its eight short verses which began:

> 'Out of the depths I cry to you O Lord
> O Lord hear my voice.
> Let your ears be attentive
> to my cry for mercy'

a warm and comforting wave of reassurance flooded over me. Suddenly I realised that I was not as lonely, scared, helpless or vulnerable as I had thought. The author of the psalm had been there before me. Some 3,000 years earlier he had experienced very similar emotions of despair to mine. He had found a route to climb out of his depths with God's help and he had signposted that route in beautiful poetry recorded for posterity in the 19th book of the Bible known simply as 'The Psalms'.

I have offered a commentary on Psalm 130 on page 3 of this book. All that needs to be said here is that this psalm really spoke to me on my first night in prison, bringing relief to my agonised feelings of being under pressure.

My discovery was not a new one. The psalms have been a source of strength, inspiration, hope and comfort for peoples of many nations and cultures for well over 100 generations. Their origins are lost in the mists of time. Some of them were written as individual prayers and poems. Others were compositions for various forms of temple and communal worship. Their authors range from great Kings of Israel such as David and Solomon, to obscure priests, poets and musicians. Between them the psalms cover just about every mood, emotion and situation known to the human spirit.

One of the unexpected benefits of my prison sentence was that for almost the first time, in a life that had been led on fast tracks at high stress levels, I had plenty of time at my disposal for reflection and reading. I soon discovered, like monks in past centuries, that a cell can be a great place to pray in. Inspired by my initial encounter with Psalm 130, I made it a regular part of my routine to ponder and pray over two or three psalms each day. The results of this discipline were amazing.

While in jail I found myself continuously grappling with an onslaught of problems. They came in three categories – immediate, external, and spiritual. The most immediate one was simply survival. I had to avoid trouble and get to know the ropes of prison life. Soon I learned how to go with the flow of the community. I began to build relationships within my fast expanding social circle. Although I was met with much kindness and gentle humour from my fellow inmates, nevertheless for me the ever-lurking challenge was coping with threats or acts of aggression. So I had to discover how to tell the difference between 'real men' and 'plastics' and how to keep my head well below the parapet with the prisoners and occasional prison officers who wanted to give me a hard time.

Although the difficulties of life in the prison community had their moments of high pressure they were, in con-speak, 'easy gravy' compared to my external difficulties. These included a constant barrage of media attacks and intrusions; family worries; financial ruin; communication problems caused by lack of phone calls; and defending myself in new litigation battles launched against me by old adversaries.

The third and hardest-to-define category of problem could be described as 'spiritual difficulties'. To put it simply, my problem was: How to stay calm and centred spiritually when outside temporal forces are battering you with blows and disasters. Prison is one of those high pressure environments in which small problems enlarge into big problems and serious problems expand in the mind into catastrophes. For a time I was brought close to breaking point by my combinations of pressures but gradually I moved into quieter waters, thanks in no small measure to the psalms.

To give one example of how a psalm lifted me out of a quagmire of despair: Just about the worst moment of my external troubles arrived in September 1999 when my creditors at the *Guardian* and Granada Television took an unprecedented legal action against me. Having used their powers under insolvency law to seize all my files of personal correspondence on the pretext of searching for hidden financial assets (none existed), they changed course and asserted that the contents of these files were 'an asset' which should be sold off for the benefit of my estate in bankruptcy. A firm of auctioneers were engaged to peruse my personal letters and to discuss their market value with various newspapers. On this basis a valuation of not less than £100,000 was placed on my correspondence, which ranged from ancient love letters to letters of political and historical interest, to up-to-date personal letters full of potentially exciting grist to the tabloid mills.

The notion that such private correspondence could be deemed an asset and sold to benefit my creditors was a novel development in the law of bankruptcy. Advised that the courts would

have to sanction it, my trustee in bankruptcy Mr Colin Haig, of
Baker Tilly, duly launched the litigation of *Haig v. Aitken,* whose
sole purpose was to legitimise the proposed sale of these alleged
'assets'. When the case was set down for trial my despairing spir-
its hit rock bottom. I could not possibly afford the cost of being
represented by counsel in the High Court. The prison Governor
refused my application for a leave pass which would have
allowed me to go to court with an escort of prison officers to
defend the case in person. So it seemed certain that my attackers
would win their action by default with the end result that my
most intimate and private letters would be sold to the highest
bidder, inevitably triggering a new round of highly embarrassing
and negative publicity for me.

In the middle of my gloom about this unfolding courtroom
drama I came across Psalm 37 which opens with the line 'Do not
fret ...'. Its first eleven verses are analysed in detail on pages 8–10
but in essence the message of the psalm is: Don't fret, don't worry,
put your trust in the Lord, commit yourself to him and he will give
your cause justice.

At this time in my prison journey I had formed a friendship
with a young Irish prisoner of great charm and vitality – Paddy
Doyle. He shared my new found interest in 'praying the psalms'
and was full of sympathy for my worries over the attempt to sell
my personal letters. Paddy, who had in him the qualities of a
good recruiting sergeant, decided that our two-man prayer part-
nership needed reinforcements to help in this crisis. So in double-
quick time he persuaded a blagger (armed robber), a dipper
(pickpocket), a kiter (fraudster), and a lifer (murderer) to join us.
This created an unusual team for praying together, so unusual
that it gave a new meaning to the Christian term 'a cell group'.
However strange its membership may have looked to outsiders,
the group was marvellously effective in getting prayers answered.
For soon after we had all prayed about the impending court case
over my letters and read Psalm 37 together, a remarkable chain
of events began to unfold. For a start I found it possible to obey
the psalm's opening exhortation, 'Do not fret'. I became peaceful
instead of worried. Trusting the Lord produced even more

extraordinary results. A young barrister unknown to me, Mr Tom Lowe, heard about the impending case of *Haig v. Aitken* and was so outraged by the issues it raised that he volunteered to defend me *pro bono*, or free of charge. A lawyer who offers to fight a case in the High Court without being paid for it was one miracle. A second was having the trial presided over by a judge with no sympathy whatever for the case my creditors tried to argue: 'I find the plaintiffs action morally repugnant' declared Mr Justice Rattee as he refused to allow the sale of my letters. My trustee in bankruptcy and his creditors committee were greatly embarrassed by his robust judgment, not to mention the hostile headlines that accompanied press reports of it. Back in our prison prayer group we agreed that verse 6 of Psalm 37, which says the Lord will make the justice of your cause shine like the noonday sun, had come gloriously true. It was the first of many good answers which came our way over the next few months from praying the psalms.

As a result of these and other experiences I often found myself asking the question: What is it about the psalms that makes their appeal so powerful? Some say it is the beautiful language of the original Hebrew poetry. Some highlight the spiritual poignancy of the psalmists' prayers. Others emphasise the psalms underlying and often repeated themes such as the earthly conflict between the forces of good and evil; the need to be constantly aware of God's mighty power; and the transcendent importance of putting our trust and hope in Him. Yet there are so many mysterious frequencies and wavelengths in the psalms that every searching soul can tune in to hear their own individually profound and personalised messages.

There was an incident right at the end of my prison sentence which served as a good illustration of the universality of appeal in the psalms. My friends in our prayer or fellowship group, as it became known (by then about twenty strong in regular membership), asked me to give a valedictory talk on Psalm 130 two weeks before my release date. The event was advertised on various notice boards. As a result the attendance swelled beyond the usual Christian suspects. Indeed there was general astonishment when just before I got up to speak we were joined in the prison chapel by no less a personage than 'The Big Face'.

Every prison has among its inmates a head honcho called 'The Big Face'. The term originally derives from the time when notorious criminals had their faces plastered up on big poster sites above the word WANTED. Nowadays it is reserved for the most feared and ferocious prisoner in a particular jail. Our Big Face was an old-style gangland boss coming towards the end of a 34-year lifer's tariff imposed on him for a string of revenge killings back in the 1960's. As the old Wild West saying has it, he was not a man to go to the well with. Indeed his unexpected arrival at our fellowship group to hear a talk on Psalm 130 made several people distinctly nervous, not least the speaker.

I began my address by saying that this psalm had made a deep impact on me throughout my prison journey starting with my first scary night as a new arrival in HMP Belmarsh. I had come to believe that it might have a great message for anyone suffering 'in the depths'. Then to improve my street credibility as an interpreter of scripture I mentioned that it was not only *my* favourite Psalm. It also happened to be the favourite psalm of Augustine, Luther and Calvin. The Big Face nodded gravely on receiving this information.

By the time I got towards the end of my interpretation of the Psalm, I noticed that The Big Face was visibly moved. In fact tears were trickling down his cheeks as he listened with deep concentration. As I finished the talk with a prayer, The Big Face joined in with a booming Amen. A few moments later he drew me aside with an unexpected request.

'Jonno that there psalm was beautiful, real beautiful. Got to me 'eart it did,' began The Big Face, 'and I want to ask you a favour. Do you think you could come over to me Peter (cell) on A wing tomorrow night and say your piece over again. I got a couple of me best mates it would mean a real lot to.'

I may have looked a little anxious at the prospect of spending an evening in the company of The Big Face and two of his closest associates. Sensing my hesitation he enlarged his invitation, 'And Jonno, to make yourself feel comfortable, why don't you bring a couple of your mates along with you,' said The Big Face graciously. 'I mean 'ow about bringing those geezers you said liked the psalm so much – Augustus and wotsits too if they're friends of yours on B wing.'

Although I was unable to produce St Augustine, Calvin and Luther as my companions, Psalm 130 went down well second time round in The Big Face's cell, with different verses appealing to different villains. Although this surprised me at the time, the more I have come to know the psalms, the less they surprise me in their power to speak to a wide variety of people and situations. How I wish I had discovered their spiritual riches earlier in life for I am certain they would have helped me enormously in coping with the numerous high pressure crises I encountered in my political, media and business careers.

After my release from prison I spent two years at Oxford studying theology at Wycliffe Hall. Towards the end of my first year I had to satisfy the University examiners in an Old Testament paper with The Psalms as my special subject. The level of academic scholarship required by this examination compelled me to acquire a wider and deeper knowledge of the Psalter which I hope I have put to good use in this book. However, it is the lessons of real life rather than of academic life which have made me venture into the role of amateur commentator on the Psalms.

Although the idea of writing a book with the title *Psalms for People Under Pressure* first came to me in prison, what has carried it forward is the realisation that many people in the world of freedom are prisoners of pressure. Modern pressures come in a multitude of forms and disguises. Unhappy lifestyles, unfulfilled careers, financial anxieties, broken relationships, professional disappointments and personal worries are just a few of the bars and chains in ordinary life which can be every bit as oppressive as the bars and chains of a real prison. Because a love of the psalms helped me to liberate and quieten my soul I hope that these thoughts on a selection of some 27 psalms will encourage others to journey down the same road in hopes of finding and strengthening their own relationship with God.

ACKNOWLEDGEMENTS

I gratefully acknowledge all those whose teaching, friendship and prayer have helped me to write this book.

They include the friends who have been my prayer partners in a Westminster based group since 1997: Michael Alison, Tom Benyon, Alastair Burt, Anthony Cordle, David Christie, Michael Hastings, James Pringle and Mervyn Thomas. They gave great encouragement to my hesitant idea of writing this book when we held a retreat based on the psalms at Burford Priory in October 2002.

I owe special thanks to my tutors at Wycliffe Hall, Oxford, when I was a resident student there in 2000–2002 reading theology, particularly Alister McGrath, Michael Green, Graham Tomlin and Philip Johnston. The latter's lectures and lecture notes were invaluable to me both as a student and as an author.

My spiritual journey with the psalms has been enriched by an extraordinarily wide range of friends. I look back with special gratitude to my prison prayer groups in HMP Belmarsh and HMP Stanford Hill in 1999–2000. It was the members of those groups with whom I first started to pray the psalms, so I warmly thank Paddy, Phil, Colin, Carl, Clinton, Christian, Rob, Geoff, Mickey, Paul, Slim, Ude, Buster, Harry, Brian, Kevin, Dave, Poncho and Antitank for being such staunch companions in prayer and Bible study.

In and around Washington DC I prayed the psalms with several friends, among them Charles W. Colson, Al Regnery, Steve Bull, Harry Hogan, Joe Johnston Jnr and Max Salas. I also have good friends among the clergy who, at various stages, have illuminated the psalms for me with their teaching and prayer, including Norman Brown, the late Michael Chantry, Philip Chester, John Collins, Richard Coombs, Paul Cowley, Nicky Gumbel, Chris Hancock, Gerard Hughes, Bishop James Jones, Dick

Lucas, Mark Roberts, Lister Tonge and Paul Zaphiriou. Other lay friends with whom I have shared thoughts and prayers on the psalms include Michael Bates, Bob Edmiston, Judy Cahusac, Judith and Martin Marriott, Tricia Neill, Zilla Hawkins, Ben Rogers, and Bruce and Geraldine Streather.

The burden of typing the manuscript was borne by the Revd Jasmine Roberts, with additional help from Helen Kirkpatrick. To both my warm thanks.

I also thank Robin Baird-Smith and his team at Continuum for their support and encouragement as my publishers.

Last but not least I acknowledge my debt to some thirty earlier commentators on the psalms whose books are listed in the bibliography on page 136. Some of them became the closest of companions on my author's journey, so my special thanks to Craig Broyles, J. H. Eaton, Derek Kidner, A. F. Kirkpatrick, C. S. Lewis, C. H. Spurgeon, John Stott and Michael Wilcock.

Finally, my greatest thanks go to my wife Elizabeth. When we were married at St Matthew's Westminster on 25 June 2003, I do not think she entirely understood why her going away trousseau was being supplemented by a large suitcase of commentaries on the psalms. Indeed, some brides might have been surprised to discover that the honeymoon in the Bahamas would be partly taken up by the bridegroom writing a book for people under pressure. But Elizabeth took it all in good heart with amusement to herself and encouragement to me. For her forbearance, sense of humour and great love my deepest gratitude.

SUGGESTIONS ON HOW
TO READ THIS BOOK

This book can be read for general interest, for literary or poetic study, for practical guidance, for spiritual searching, or for use in prayer.

I have kept all these possible approaches in mind when writing *Psalms for People Under Pressure*. However, my primary purpose has been to help others to discover the spiritual riches of the psalms.

The psalms are falling out of fashion in contemporary religious practice. Although there are still cathedrals, churches and religious orders which maintain the discipline of saying or singing the psalms as part of the daily office, these are now the exception rather than the rule. So an unfamiliarity gap has opened up between God's psalms and God's people. It is a gap that can be bridged by searching for a better understanding of the relevance of the psalms to our spiritual needs and lives in the 21st century.

To those who are pursuing this quest by reading this book, I recommend taking it slowly at the rate of one, or at the most two, psalms a day. I suggest that each one should be read through twice before moving on to the Reflection passage which is intended to illustrate the message of every psalm.

The additional notes which follow aim to explain difficult verses or phrases. Sometimes they highlight points of history or theology but more often these apparently rather technical points offer spiritual insight that derive from an initially obscure part of the psalm.

The third section of observations on each psalm is a personal comment. At the risk of falling into the excesses of egotism I have tried to explain how the psalm helped me or spoke to me at a particular moment in my life. Every reader will have their own personal responses to a psalm. Mine are nothing special but they may act as examples of how an ancient psalm can connect with modern life.

Fourthly, I have offered at the end of my commentaries on each psalm a prayer based on it. These prayers may have erred on the side of brevity but perhaps they will act as a stimulus to other people's deeper efforts in that wonderful spiritual endeavour known as 'praying the psalms'.

Finally, I should make it clear that this book has been created on the basis of a highly personal selection process. At least three-quarters of the Bible's 150 psalms could qualify for the description of *Psalms for People Under Pressure*. So I have had to make difficult choices, hence the title for Part I of the book's contents 'The Top Ten Psalms for People Under Pressure'. This runs the risk of sounding like Desert Island Discs, but at least it makes clear the subjectivity, perhaps even the idiosyncrasy, of my selections, as does the title of Part II, 'Special Situations of Pressure'.

As for the title of Part III, 'Understanding God When Under Pressure', this is almost an impertinence. For his ways are not our ways and we are usually blind to his mysterious purposes. I agree with Job who said the best we could do towards understanding God was to see *the outskirts of his ways* (Job 26: 14). Yet I have come to believe that the psalms give us some of the best glimpses of understanding into those outskirts. Perhaps this is why the psalms have been such a powerful source of spiritual comfort down the ages. For they have inspired not only the original Israelites who first used them to worship God, but also many generations of Christian believers as well as numerous followers of other faiths. May this small book help others in our time to join the long tradition of reading, praying and loving the psalms.

PART I

THE TOP TEN PSALMS FOR PEOPLE UNDER PRESSURE

PSALM 130: Out of the depths

A song of ascents.

Out of the depths I cry to you, O Lord;
  [2] O Lord, hear my voice.
Let your ears be attentive
  to my cry for mercy.

[3] If you, O Lord, kept a record of sins,
  O Lord, who could stand?
[4] But with you there is forgiveness;
  therefore you are feared.

[5] I wait for the Lord, my soul waits,
  and in his word I put my hope.
[6] My soul waits for the Lord
  more than watchmen wait for the morning,
  more than watchmen wait for the morning.

[7] O Israel, put your hope in the Lord,
  for with the Lord is unfailing love
  and with him is full redemption.
[8] He himself will redeem Israel
  from all their sins.

REFLECTION

All of us sink into the depths at some stage in our lives. At its best this experience puts us under pressure. At its worst the descent drags us down into depression and despair. There can even be times when, like Hamlet in his 'sea of troubles', our depths become so overwhelming that we contemplate suicide. A test for troubled souls at such moments is to ask whether we are prepared to face the realisation that there may be no man-made powers such as self-help or self-will that can haul us out of our depths.

This psalm signposts a spiritual route for climbing out of the depths with the help of God's power. It identifies six milestones along the route. They are: crying; surrendering to God; seeking his forgiveness; waiting; hoping; and receiving his gifts of unfailing love and full redemption.

Crying (verse 1) may sometimes mean tears but it always means prayers. A loving God hears and responds to requests made to him with the sincerity of a praying heart. We may have to persevere with our prayers and shape them to accord with his will. But the first step is to open up the channel of communication to God by crying or praying to him. The familiar expression 'if you're in a hole stop digging' should be amended in the light of this psalm to 'if you're in a hole start praying'.

The prayer should be a *cry for mercy* (verse 2) coupled with a recognition of our need to surrender to God with a plea for his forgiveness. The 19th century Baptist preacher C. H. Spurgeon said that verses 3 and 4 contained 'the essence of all scripture'. He was right. For a journey out of the depths must begin with the recognition that our human frailties allow no-one to stand before God in self-justification. He is always ready to offer us the cleansing power of his forgiveness (verse 4) and the new start to our lives that should follow. However, the old fashioned words at the end of the verse *therefore you are feared* (verse 4) should make us think. In this context they mean that the God who forgives us and pulls us out of the depths should be put at the centre of our lives in a new relationship of loving reverence and respect. To those who quibble that this is not the same as fearing, these further words from C. H. Spurgeon may give the answer 'None fear the Lord like those who have experienced his forgiving love'.

Only in the soft option world of synthetic spirituality is the process of receiving God's forgiveness and entering into a new relationship with him a quick fix. Climbing out of the depths may take time, possibly a long time. After sinning against God restoring fellowship with him can sometimes be a slow and painful process. As if to underline this problem the psalm moves on to the eloquent verses about patience (5–6), for how and why we wait for God's will to be done are two profoundly important issues to be resolved on our journey out of the depths.

Spiritual patience is one of the hardest virtues to achieve. Using the Hebrew poetic devise of parallelism (double repetition) the psalmist highlights this difficulty by using the imagery of watchmen yearning for daybreak (verse 6). Yet behind this reminder that God's timing may not be our timing lies a promise of a new life, which like the arrival of morning itself, will definitely dawn. The soul marooned in the depths is advised to wait with patience but to hope with certainty. The hope lies in God's word (verse 5) and in his promises.

The final verses (7–8) advise the committed people of God (Israel) to hope and trust that they will receive the divine reward for those who pray and wait patiently in their depths. That reward is defined as God's *unfailing love and full redemption* (verse 7). It includes a liberation from the burden of all past sins, (verse 8) and a new life obeying God's will.

The climb out of the depths may be a long haul and at times a painful one. I found it so. Yet I am one of a multitude of readers and pray-ers of this great psalm who know that its guidance is right and that its promises are true.

ADDITIONAL NOTES

Title: This is the eleventh of fifteen psalms (120–134) which bears the title *A song of ascents*. Most scholars believe they were a collection of pilgrimage poems sung by worshippers going up to Jerusalem to attend one or other of the three annual festivals celebrated in the temple.

Form: In the Christian tradition this is classified as one of the seven penitential psalms (the others are 6, 32, 38, 51, 102 and 143) because the author's individual experience of penitence and forgiveness leads him to urge Israel, corporately, to trust God for redemption. Luther classified it as one of the 'Pauline Psalms' (the others he so named were 51, 32 and 143) because it offers forgiveness by grace without works. Luther was one of several Christian figures who have said that Psalm 130 was their favourite psalm. Others include Augustine of Hippo, John Calvin, John Bunyan and C. H. Wesley.

Verse 1: *cry*: Some translations use 'call' but in this context both words are a synonym for 'pray'. Augustine of Hippo's comment on this verse was: 'When we cry to our Lord from the depths he heareth our cry and the very cry itself suffereth us to move from the bottom.' (1)

Verse 4: *Therefore you are feared*: John Stott has made this comment: 'Fear and love are the inseparable elements of true religion. Fear preserves love from degenerating into presumptuous familiarity. Love prevents fear from becoming a servile and cringing dread.' (2)

Verses 7–8: After six verses as an individual psalm, the author changes tone to exhort Israel corporately. Some scholars have argued that these final verses are a later addition. A more plausible speculation is that an individual cantor led the pilgrims first in prayer to God, then in testimony, and finally in corporate worship.

Verse 7: *full redemption* is more beautifully rendered as *plenteous redemption* by Miles Coverdale, who translated the psalms for the *Book of Common Prayer*.

PERSONAL COMMENT

As described in the Preface (see page xvi) I first came across Psalm 130 in a meaningful way when I was paralysed with fear in my prison cell on the first night of my sentence. It spoke to me with such reassurance that I prayed over it every single day of my imprisonment, sometimes sharing it with my fellow inmates (see page xx).

After my release I continued sharing my thoughts on this psalm as a Christian public speaker. My audiences have included politicians in Washington DC; persecuted underground churches in China; powerful financiers in the City of London; prisoners in Mississippi; and parishioners in churches around the world.

One of the most responsive groups I have ever addressed on Psalm 130 was the staff of the White House. I was invited there to talk to what I thought was a tiny Christian fellowship circle, but to my amazement some sixty of President Bush's top staffers turned out to discuss this psalm. Their questions and comments left me humbled, for as I should have known the pressures of power can be an 'in the depths' experience. Yet I was also uplifted by the confirmation that this psalm has a huge universality of spiritual appeal. Looking back on my own depths I now realise that there are many other dramas in life's journey which are far harder to bear than a prison sentence, not least because they have no certain release dates. Such depths include bereavement, serious illness, depression, unemployment, personal failure, public humiliation and broken relationships. They can all be helped by studying and praying this great psalm.

A SHORT PRAYER BASED ON PSALM 130

O Lord hear my prayer for mercy and help me climb out of my depths. Guide me so that I may learn how to surrender my will to yours. Show me how to accept your offer of forgiveness. Teach me how to bear my time in the depths with patience and with hope in your word. In your mercy grant me the great blessings of your unfailing love and full redemption. Through Jesus Christ Our Lord. Amen.

PSALM 37: Verses 1–11. Do not fret

Of David.

Do not fret because of evil men
  or be envious of those who do wrong;
[2] for like the grass they will soon wither,
  like green plants they will soon die away.

[3] Trust in the Lord and do good;
  dwell in the land and enjoy safe pasture.
[4] Delight yourself in the Lord
  and he will give you the desires of your heart.
[5] Commit your way to the Lord;
  trust in him and he will do this:
[6] He will make your righteousness shine like the dawn,
  the justice of your cause like the noonday sun.

[7] Be still before the Lord and wait patiently for him;
  do not fret when men succeed in their ways,
  when they carry out their wicked schemes.

[8] Refrain from anger and turn from wrath;
  do not fret – it leads only to evil.
[9] For evil men will be cut off,
  but those who hope in the Lord will inherit the land.

[10] A little while, and the wicked will be no more;
  though you look for them, they will not be found.
[11] But the meek will inherit the land
  and enjoy great peace.

REFLECTION

Worry is the cause of most pressure. The opening verses of this psalm contain a series of important spiritual instructions. If we follow them we may discover the secret of how to avoid worry; how to avoid getting hot under the collar; and how to find inner peace.

Do not fret (verse 1) is the opening command. For most of us it is easier said than done, particularly if we're coming under attack in unfair ways from unpleasant people. But the psalmist presses his point. Stop worrying about the bad guys, he advises. Don't envy them or their ill-gotten gains and successes (verses 1 and 8). Their triumphs are temporary. They will wither away like dry grass (verse 2).

The psalm develops its message with three positive exhortations. *Trust in the Lord* (verse 3). *Delight yourself in the Lord* (verse 4). *Commit your way to the Lord* (verse 5).

Trusting is one of the surest keys to a right relationship with God. Pressure hits everyone sooner or later, particularly when things are going wrong. But they will not go wrong in a way that will break the relationship or profoundly disappoint us, provided we keep our spiritual batteries charged with Godly trust. This requires commitment at all times, and will delight us in good times. For God's blessings give his trusting and committed people great joy. This is why so many of the psalms round off with a crescendo of thanksgiving and rejoicing.

Those whose selfish and sometimes unscrupulously achieved successes are limited to the time horizons of the present may seem to be running off with life's glittering prizes. But don't get angry or envious about them, repeats the psalmist (verses 7 and 8). Those bad guys have not grasped the concept of eternity. They can't see that they're soon for the chop. They have cut themselves off (verse 9a) from the riches of eternal life, whereas those who trust and put their hope in the Lord will inherit the land (verse 9b).

A worldly sceptic belonging to the 'I want it now' school of materialism might argue that this promise of an inheritance of spiritual riches is a mirage. So how do we discern the difference between a worldly mirage and a Godly oasis, particularly at a time when worries and pressures are piling in on us? One answer can be found in the four words at the beginning of verse 7: *Be still before the Lord*. It is a command that is repeated many times in the Bible, perhaps most notably in Psalm 46 verse 10: *Be still and know that I am God*. In terms of prayer this means keeping the discipline of setting aside some regular quiet time for listening to and communing with God. As a later psalm reflected on in this book, Psalm 73, tells us, there will come a moment when we will understand why the wicked don't matter. What matters to those keeping faith with God are the trust, delight, and commitment imperatives the psalmist urges us to obey.

These verses of Psalm 37 open by offering an antidote to worry and close with a promise of peace. The lovely words of verse 11: *The meek will inherit the land and enjoy great peace* were used by Jesus as the basis for his fifth beatitude in the sermon on the mount; 'Blessed are the meek for they shall inherit the earth' (Matthew 5: 5). Who are these fortunate people, the meek? One answer might be that they are those who have humbly and obediently followed the teachings of this psalm.

ADDITIONAL NOTES

Title and Form: Of David: This superscription is applied to 73 of the 150 psalms in the Bible. There is much speculation by scholars over the question that arises from this titular genitive. Was David the author of them all? Or were they written by court and other poets for the use of the Davidic monarch and his line? The answer is that there are plenty of examples of both categories. Psalm 37 is more likely to have been written by a professional poet since it is an acrostic psalm. This is an elaborate technical structure, in which each of the full psalm's 22 stanzas start with the 22 letters of the Hebrew alphabet: i.e., the first word of the first stanza begins with *aleph*, the second stanza begins with *beth* and so on.

The use of the acrostic technique emphasises that this is a Wisdom psalm. It was probably used in schools as part of the curriculum of ancient Israel's moral and religious education system.

Acrostic psalms have their limitations in terms of poetic thought but the alphabetic structure made them easy to memorise in schools or in temple worship.

Verse 1: *Do not fret*: The literal translation from the Hebrew is 'do not get heated about'. This verse is taken almost verbatim from Proverbs 24: 19.

Verses 5–6: *Commit*: See also Proverbs 16: 3.

Righteousness: There is an implication here and in the succeeding verses that the righteous may have to wait for justice but God will vindicate them and honour his promises. See Matthew 13: 43.

Verse 8: *Anger*: Means both anger against the wicked and anger against God.

Verse 11: *Meek*: See Matthew 5: 5 and Reflection.

The Psalm as a whole: The psalm as a whole can seem repetitious for the entire 40 verses do little more than reiterate the theme of the first 11. However, the contrasts between the fates of the righteous and the wicked are illuminated by several eye witness insights from the psalmist, particularly in verses 25, 35 and 36.

PERSONAL COMMENT

I used to be a great worrier. I have not managed to eliminate this habit completely but I have reduced it substantially as a result of learning from this psalm.

In the Preface (see pages xvii–xviii) I described how praying over Psalm 37 with a group of fellow prisoners managed to transform a major worry into a major victory. Here is another example of help given to me by this psalm a few months later.

Like many ex-prisoners I found the early weeks after release a difficult period of adjustment. Somehow I had thought that once I had 'paid my debt to society' life would be easier. Not so. Within a month or so of leaving prison I came under pressure from a new onslaught of newspaper attacks. The gist of them was that I was withholding millions of pounds from my creditors, concealed in a secret Swiss bank account. The allegations were untrue as I eventually proved. But at the time the stories made unpleasant reading.

On the day when the worst of these allegations were published, I went to an evening service at Holy Trinity Brompton, the London church where I had done an Alpha course some months earlier. The service was taken by The Revd Nicky Gumbel, the Alpha Chaplain, whose teachings had helped me enormously. Towards the end of the evening Nicky invited all those who wanted to be prayed for to come forward.

At that time I had not entirely lost the instincts of a traditional member of the church-reticent wing of Anglicanism. The idea of coming forward in public in this way turned me off. But my need was stronger than my reluctance. So with heavy leaden footsteps I did go forward for the first time in my life to be prayed for.

When I reached the front of the church Nicky Gumbel saw me and asked what my prayer need was. In ten seconds I summarised the problem. Nicky thumbed through his Bible and read me the first few verses of Psalm 37. They struck a strong chord in my memory. Although my worries did not fade away overnight, I calmed down. Within a few weeks my Trustee in Bankruptcy established that the Swiss bank account named and numbered in the newspaper story had no connection with me. A public statement to the effect that I had not concealed any assets was made later by the Trustee. Perhaps it was not quite as good as making my righteousness shine like the dawn (verse 6) but this vindication certainly paved the way for the annulment of my bankruptcy by agreement of all creditors.

I have taken my experiences of Psalm 37 to heart. These days when I start to get het up with worry I try to remember the three exhortations contained in verses 3, 4, and 5: Trust in the Lord … Delight in the Lord … Commit to the Lord. My mnemonic for this are the initials TDC, which I find easy to recall because during my 23 years as Member of Parliament for Thanet I wrote several letters each day to the Thanet District Council!

Whatever method is used for praying this psalm, its opening verses are a classic statement of faith. Its message can be a great help to anyone under pressure from worry.

A SHORT PRAYER BASED ON PSALM 37

Heavenly Father, help me to put aside my cares or worries and concentrate on you. I trust you. I delight in you. I commit my life to you. Stop me from hating or envying those who do wrong. In the stillness of my prayers guide me to the blessings of your peace. Through Jesus Christ Our Lord. Amen.

PSALM 91: God's protection

He who dwells in the shelter of the Most High
    will rest in the shadow of the Almighty.
[2] I will say of the Lord, 'He is my refuge and my fortress,
    my God, in whom I trust.'

[3] Surely he will save you from the fowler's snare
    and from the deadly pestilence.
[4] He will cover you with his feathers,
    and under his wings you will find refuge;
    his faithfulness will be your shield and rampart.
[5] You will not fear the terror of night,
    nor the arrow that flies by day,
[6] nor the pestilence that stalks in the darkness,
    nor the plague that destroys at midday.
[7] A thousand may fall at your side,
    ten thousand at your right hand,
    but it will not come near you.
[8] You will only observe with your eyes
    and see the punishment of the wicked.

[9] If you make the Most High your dwelling –
    even the Lord, who is my refuge –
[10] then no harm will befall you,
    no disaster will come near your tent.
[11] For he will command his angels concerning you
    to guard you in all your ways;
[12] they will lift you up in their hands,
    so that you will not strike your foot against a stone.
[13] You will tread upon the lion and the cobra;
    you will trample the great lion and the serpent.

[14] 'Because he loves me,' says the Lord, 'I will rescue him;
    I will protect him, for he acknowledges my name.
[15] He will call upon me, and I will answer him;
    I will be with him in trouble,
    I will deliver him and honour him.

[16] With long life will I satisfy him
    and show him my salvation.'

REFLECTION

This is a psalm about God's protection over those who love him.
At times its poetic imagery overflows into poetic licence with the
sweeping grandeur of the guaranteed protection described by the
psalmist. When the Lord himself speaks in the final stanza the
promises are more carefully defined. If we reflect spiritually
about both the poetry and the promises this can be a psalm of
assurance and comfort to people under pressure.

The psalm has a majestic opening that contains four names for
God and four metaphors describing the security he provides –
shelter, shadow, refuge and fortress (verses 1 and 2).

In the next eleven verses the psalmist portrays a celestial insurance policy which is so comprehensive that its underwriters
would have to be angels. The faithful believer is offered protection against plots and entrapments (*the fowler's snare* – verse 3);
disease or pestilence (verses 3 and 6); night-time terrors; daily
accidents and epidemics of the plague (verses 5 and 6).

The personal cover of the insurance policy expands still further
in verses 7–13. Even if ten thousand of the insured's neighbours
die from the plague he will not be infected (verse 7). No disaster
or harm will come his way if he treads on lions or poisonous
snakes (verse 13). Angels will always be on hand to guard him
from even the smallest misfortune such as stubbing his toe
against a stone (verses 11–12).

Some of these miraculous deliverances were granted to the people of Israel by the God of the Old Testament during the Exodus.
This is the source of the psalmist's inspiration for his poetic
imagery. However, the contemporary reader must beware the
impression that praying this psalm offers the spiritual equivalent
of a blank cheque. Indeed, some faithful believers who have been
innocent victims of accidents or illness may find the poetic licence
of these verses fanciful if not cruel.

So there are parts of this psalm which should not be taken literally, among them the implication in verse 15 that disease is the punishment of the wicked. Yet, if we look carefully at the last three verses of the psalm which set out God's version of his protection, the insurance cover is narrower but more reassuring.

The key to the protection is the individual's relationship with God. It has to be built on love, fidelity and prayer. A change of voice enters the psalm at verse 14 to say this. It is the voice of the Lord himself who declares:

Because he loves me I will rescue him.
I will protect him for he acknowledges my name
He will call upon me and I will answer him.
I will be with him in trouble
I will deliver him and honour him (verses 14–15).

Unlike the poet who composed the imaginative verses in the early part of the psalm, God is a God of reality. He knows that we all go through periods of trouble in our lives. He does not promise to deliver from adversity. He promises to deliver us in adversity. He will come alongside us with answers (verse 15) but not necessarily with the miracles of the Exodus. Nevertheless his offer includes deliverance, honour, long life (which also means eternal life), satisfaction and salvation. These are far richer rewards than earthly protection.

ADDITIONAL NOTES

Form and Title: This is a psalm of encouragement and instruction. It falls into two parts. In the first part (verses 1-13) two voices speak or sing antiphonally. In the second part (verses 14-16) God is the speaker. As there is no title, there are no clues to the authorship. Kirkpatrick and other scholars have suggested that the first part could be a dialogue between David and Solomon.

Verse 1: *Most High*: 'a title that cuts every threat down to size,' says Kidner (3).

Almighty: the name used by the early patriarchs for Yahweh. Both are synonyms of God and go back to the days of Abraham (Genesis 14: 18 ff; 17: 1; Exodus 6: 3).

Verse 3: *Fowler's snare*: Trap set by hunters of birds but the threat is metaphorical.

Verse 7: *A thousand may fall*: May be a reference to battles or to the plagues that often broke out among soldiers on military campaigns.

Verses 11 and 12: These verses have the unusual distinction of being quoted by the devil. See the Gospel accounts of the temptation of Christ; Matthew 4: 6; Luke 4: 10-11. However, Satan completely misapplied the psalm which read in its entirety does not promise unconditional security in every circumstance. See Reflection.

Verses 14–16: This is a divine oracle. God's promises from the voice of God. Such a change of voice is heard in other psalms such as 60: 6–8; 81: 6–16; and 95: 8–12.

PERSONAL COMMENT

Relatively early in my spiritual journey (i.e., before the libel case trial which led to my imprisonment) I was advised to pray this psalm for protection. I did and it failed me – or so I thought. So for a time I took rather a negative view of the psalmist's over the top claims in the first thirteen verses, even though the poetry with which they are described is magnificent.

Now I understand the psalm better I can see that it did not fail me. I failed God. It is all explained in this line: *Because he loves me,* says the Lord, *I will rescue him* (verse 14). How does God know if the person praying for protection loves Him? One test is that if you love him you will keep his commandments (John 14: 15). I did not, so no wonder the psalmist's prayer for protection was no help at that time.

The message of this psalm is echoed by St Paul in Romans 8: 28: *In all things God works for the good of those who love him.* That does not of course mean an absence of all trouble. It means that God will be with you in trouble. By the time I found out how to love God, he was with me.

A PRAYER BASED ON PSALM 91

Almighty God, my only true saviour and protector, shelter me in your fortress of refuge when I am in harm's way. Send your angels to guard me against the snares, arrows and pestilences of this hostile world. When I pray to you in my time of trouble answer me and save me. For I love you and honour your holy name. Through Jesus Christ Our Lord. Amen.

PSALM 121: Keeping watch over our pressures

A song of ascents.

I lift up my eyes to the hills –
  where does my help come from?
[2] My help comes from the Lord,
  the Maker of heaven and earth.

[3] He will not let your foot slip –
  he who watches over you will not slumber;
[4] indeed, he who watches over Israel
  will neither slumber nor sleep.

[5] The Lord watches over you –
  the Lord is your shade at your right hand;
[6] the sun will not harm you by day,
  nor the moon by night.

[7] The Lord will keep you from all harm –
  he will watch over your life;
[8] the Lord will watch over your coming and going
  both now and for evermore.

REFLECTION

This psalm is a powerful and beautiful expression of faith in God's vigilance. Like Psalm 91 it is a poem not a blank cheque. The pilgrims of ancient Israel who sang it on their way up to Jerusalem over two thousand years ago did not literally expect to be preserved from every single pitfall and danger on their journey any more than we should expect to travel through life free from pain, trouble or pressure. What we can count on is God's watchful presence alongside us on our journey.

The psalm opens on an apprehensive note. Those hills (verse 1) the author was lifting up his eyes to were full of perils, among them bandits, wild animals, and slippery paths. So he asks the question *where does my help come from?* (verse 2) and receives the stunning answer that the creator of the universe will be his helper.

The belief that God the creator also uses his awesome power to watch over our individual lives with ceaseless vigilance is emphasised even more powerfully in the original Hebrew than in any English translation. For the same Hebrew word is repeated six times in four verses to drive home the message that God will be our keeper at all times. This is a watchman who *will neither slumber nor sleep* (verse 4) and shade us from burning heat and blinding light. The sun and the moon (verse 6) were often worshipped as false gods in ancient times. These misguided practices have plenty of 21st century equivalents, among them the worship of money; the idolising of celebrity; or the devotion to beauty, health and fitness. Such obsessions can easily burn us or blind us but God is always there to offer the cool shade of spiritual refreshment and protection.

Only God can keep watch over all the comings and goings of our lives. He will do this *now and for evermore* (verse 8). This wonderful coupling of the immediate and the everlasting lifts the psalmist's vision beyond the horizons of time. His message is that God's protective surveillance covers every moment of a soul's journey – from here to eternity.

ADDITIONAL NOTES

Form and Title: *A Song of Ascent* (see note on Psalm 130).

Psalm 121 appears to have been written for antiphonal chanting. The question in verse 1 gets an answer in verse 2, while verses 3–4 may be a greeting or parting blessing bestowed on the pilgrims by a temple priest. The tenor of the psalm suggests it might have been a regular processional or ceremonial song in cultic worship, which the scholar S. G. Mowinckel argues is a common feature in all 150 psalms.

Verse 6: *sun and moon*: The desire for protection against the sun is obvious. Less well known is that the moon was feared as a deity whose displeasure could have all sorts of adverse effects. This superstition was still going strong in the time of William Shakespeare (1564–1616) who wrote in *A Midsummer Night's Dream*:

'The moon, the governess of floods
Pale in her anger, washes all the air
That rheumatic diseases do abound.' (4)

Verse 8: beautifully translated by Coverdale as: 'The Lord shall preserve thy going out and thy coming in: from this time forth for evermore' is sometimes thought to refer to life's rites of passage from birth to death. This is one reason why Psalm 121 is often used at funerals. However, the psalmist clearly meant this final verse to have a far more sweeping and all encompassing meaning, for 'evermore' is eternity.

PERSONAL COMMENT

I can remember being moved to tears by Psalm 121 at the funeral in a West London Synagogue of my dear friend and solicitor Lord Goodman. As the cantor lead the congregation antiphonally it seemed extraordinary that we were saying farewell to this great Jewish statesman and lawyer in the style and the words that had inspired the pilgrims of Israel struggling through the hills towards Jerusalem to worship Yahweh three millennia earlier.

The line of the hymn that followed, 'A thousand ages in thy sight are like an evening gone' suddenly seemed very true and real.

On a lighter note I enjoy the story of the great editor of the *Guardian,* C. P. Scott, ordering his equally great music and cricket correspondent Neville Cardus to stop using the word 'whence' in his articles. 'There is no such word as "whence" in the English language,' insisted Scott.

Quoting Coverdale's translation from the *Book of Common Prayer* of the opening verse of Psalm 121, Cardus had the last word: 'But what about "I will lift up mine eyes to the hills from *whence* cometh my help?",' he objected. Collapse of stout editor! (5).

A PRAYER BASED ON PSALM 121

Heavenly Father, when I look at all the perils and dangers that surround me, help me to know that it is only you my Lord and creator who will watch over me and keep me from slipping into harm's way, now and for evermore. Amen.

PSALMS 42 and 43: Down and depressed

Psalm 42
For the director of music. A maskil of the Sons of Korah.

As the deer pants for streams of water,
    so my soul pants for you, O God.
[2] My soul thirsts for God, for the living God.
    When can I go and meet with God?
[3] My tears have been my food
    day and night,
while men say to me all day long,
    'Where is your God?'
[4] These things I remember
    as I pour out my soul:
how I used to go with the multitude,
    leading the procession to the house of God,
with shouts of joy and thanksgiving
    among the festive throng.

[5] Why are you downcast, O my soul?
    Why so disturbed within me?
Put your hope in God,
    for I will yet praise him,
    my Saviour and [6] my God.

My soul is downcast within me;
    therefore I will remember you
from the land of the Jordan,
    the heights of Hermon – from Mount Mizar.
[7] Deep calls to deep
    in the roar of your waterfalls;
all your waves and breakers
    have swept over me.

[8] By day the Lord directs his love,
    at night his song is with me –
    a prayer to the God of my life.
[9] I say to God my Rock,

'Why have you forgotten me?
Why must I go about mourning,
    oppressed by the enemy?'
[10] My bones suffer mortal agony
    as my foes taunt me,
saying to me all day long,
    'Where is your God?'

[11] Why are you downcast, O my soul?
    Why so disturbed within me?
Put your hope in God,
    for I will yet praise him,
    my Saviour and my God.

Psalm 43

Vindicate me, O God,
    and plead my cause against an ungodly nation;
    rescue me from deceitful and wicked men.
[2] You are God my stronghold.
    Why have you rejected me?
Why must I go about mourning,
    oppressed by the enemy?
[3] Send forth your light and your truth,
    let them guide me;
let them bring me to your holy mountain,
    to the place where you dwell.
[4] Then will I go to the altar of God,
    to God, my joy and my delight.
I will praise you with the harp,
    O God, my God.

[5] Why are you downcast, O my soul?
    Why so disturbed within me?
Put your hope in God,
    for I will yet praise him,
    my Saviour and my God.

REFLECTION

We all go through periods of feeling down and depressed. The author of these two beautiful psalms (originally written as one) was going through a particularly bad experience of depression. Yet he faced up to his troubles by asking questions with a courageous realism which lead him towards the life-giving waters of spiritual comfort.

One way of reading the sixteen verses of these psalms is to use them as a guide for how to cope with feeling down. There are three parts to this guide. In contemporary language one might call them: letting it all hang out; facing reality; and getting in touch with God.

This psalmist was not afraid to let all the symptoms of his depression hang out. He could not stop crying (42: 3). He felt totally overwhelmed by his problems which he compares to waterfalls, waves and breakers sweeping over him (42: 7). He thought he was being rejected by a forgetful God and coming under pressure from mocking men (43: 2). He was feeling the pain of past memories and present loneliness (42: 4–5). All this added up to a depression, although he used two other words beginning with 'd' – downcast and disturbed – to describe it.

Depressed people often wallow in self pity. Sometimes they seek solace in false escape routes such as alcohol or drugs. Or they become self-indulgent. As Dr Martin Lloyd Jones wrote in his book *Spiritual Depression* (6), 'We allow ourselves to talk to us rather than us talking to ourselves.' This sufferer did not make that mistake. He had a different approach. He confronted his problems. Three times he asked himself the hard question: *Why are you so downcast O my soul? Why so disturbed within me?* (42: 5, 42: 11, 43: 5)

The fact that the psalmist's self-questioning began with an analysis of the state of his soul showed that he had identified the ultimate key to all happiness. It is our relationship with God. This man, in C. S. Lewis' phrase, had a keen 'appetite for God'. In his poetry he compared himself to a deer panting and thirsting for running streams of water. His life depended on finding it. So in a three-fold refrain he urged himself; *Put your hope in God* (42: 5; 42: 11; 43: 5).

The cure for depression is not to look retrospectively to our past or introspectively at our problems, but to search for the living God. If we put our hope in him, he hears our prayers and answers them, although not always in the way or in the timescale that we are expecting.

Sometimes when we are thirsty for God he tests us and puts us through great pain. Jesus on the cross went through this agonising process; *I am thirsty* (John 19: 28) he said. His *cri de coeur* was for more than water. He was thirsting for God, thirsting to do his will even unto death.

Although the psalmist was in a drought of depression, his thirst to know God's will enabled him to look beyond the immediate emotional threshold of his troubles. He was rising above the burden of his past memories and present discomforts. He was determined to change from a self-pity-er to a self-starter. By courageously questioning himself and appealing to God, he was taking the first steps of the spiritual journey towards recovery. That journey, open to all who feel the pangs of divine thirst, leads to the living water that refreshes every need. It is a gift of grace from the loving God who heals depression and all other pains of the heart and soul.

ADDITIONAL NOTES

Title and form: Psalm 43 has no title. Its absence, and the common refrain of verses and phrases from Psalm 42 are the main reasons why most scholars believe that these are a single psalm.

A Maskil is an unknown musical term, which some translators render as 'a psalm of understanding'.

The Sons of Korah were descendants of a rebel leader of the Levites whose children were spared when he was executed for his rebellion (Numbers 26: 10). One part of Korah's family became temple doorkeepers (1 Chronicles 9: 17) and another part became singers and musicians in the choir of the temple.

42 Verse 4: *Leading the procession to the house of God:* A reference to the role played by the Korahites in temple ceremonies. The psalmist's memories of his *shouts of joy and thanksgiving among the festive throng* are in stark contrast with his present feelings of loneliness and isolation. He was evidently homesick.

42 Verse 6: *Mount Mizar:* An unidentified peak in the range around Mount Hermon in the area of upper Jordan. It is several hundred miles north of the temple in Jerusalem. Some scholars suggest that the psalmist may have been exiled in the north and forbidden to travel south to Jerusalem by the royal edict of King Jeroboam after the schism between Israel and Judah circa 930 BC. Whatever the historical background, part of the psalmist's depression was caused by loneliness and physical isolation.

43 verse 1: *Vindicate me:* This is a prayer expressed in the language of the heavenly court (*cf.* Psalm 7: 7 *et seq.*)

43 verse 4: *the altar* and *the harp:* References to the psalmist's days as a temple musician.

PERSONAL COMMENT

I have made so many mistakes in my life that going back over old ground with the wisdom of hindsight can be unbearable. Perhaps ex-politicians are particularly vulnerable to this tendency. Almost everyone in politics would have risen higher or stayed in power longer *if only...* Once we start to use those last two words too often we can be heading for the sort of depression described in these psalms.

When I was a teenager the great hit musical of the 1950s was *Salad Days* which contained a poignant song with these lyrics:

'And if you should happen to find me
 With an outlook dreary and black
 I'll remind you to remind me
 "You said you wouldn't look back." ' (7).

This is good advice. The poet who wrote Psalms 42 and 43 would have done well to heed it. He spent too much time looking back. I don't. This is because in the depths of my worst depressions when I had lost everything I started to search for God in penitence and faith. He came rushing out to welcome me, as he does with all his prodigal sons. After that, the landscape of my life changed completely. As a result I now understand what St Paul meant when he wrote these great words: *I consider everything as loss compared to the surpassing greatness of knowing Jesus Christ my Lord.* (Philippians 3: 8) A good relationship with the Lord is the cure for all depression.

A PRAYER BASED ON PSALMS 42 AND 43

Why are you so downcast O my soul? Why so disturbed within me?

Lord, in my times of depression, give me the strength to reach out to you in penitence, confidence, and faith. You are my rock, the source of the living water that will refresh my parched soul. So I pray to you in hope and trust for you are my Lord, my God and my Saviour. Come to me quickly now and rescue me! Through Jesus Christ our Lord. Amen.

PSALM 51 verses 1–17: Pressure from guilt

For the director of music. A psalm of David. When the prophet Nathan came to him after David had committed adultery with Bathsheba.

Have mercy on me, O God,
　　according to your unfailing love;
according to your great compassion
　　blot out my transgressions.
[2] Wash away all my iniquity
　　and cleanse me from my sin.

[3] For I know my transgressions,
　　and my sin is always before me.
[4] Against you, you only, have I sinned
　　and done what is evil in your sight,
so that you are proved right when you speak
　　and justified when you judge.
[5] Surely I was sinful at birth,
　　sinful from the time my mother conceived me.
[6] Surely you desire truth in the inner parts;
　　you teach me wisdom in the inmost place.

[7] Cleanse me with hyssop, and I shall be clean;
　　wash me, and I shall be whiter than snow.
[8] Let me hear joy and gladness;
　　let the bones you have crushed rejoice.
[9] Hide your face from my sins
　　and blot out all my iniquity.

[10] Create in me a pure heart, O God,
　　and renew a steadfast spirit within me.
[11] Do not cast me from your presence
　　or take your Holy Spirit from me.
[12] Restore to me the joy of your salvation
　　and grant me a willing spirit, to sustain me.

[13] Then I will teach transgressors your ways,
   and sinners will turn back to you.
[14] Save me from bloodguilt, O God,
   the God who saves me,
   and my tongue will sing of your righteousness.
[15] O Lord, open my lips,
   and my mouth will declare your praise.
[16] You do not delight in sacrifice, or I would bring it;
   you do not take pleasure in burnt offerings.
[17] The sacrifices of God are a broken spirit;
   a broken and contrite heart,
   O God, you will not despise.

REFLECTION

This is one of the greatest psalms. It tells the inner story of a king under pressure from the guilt of his terrible wickedness. Yet the voice of his conscience leads him towards a profound and penitent intimacy with God, which in turn leads to inner transformation.

The title of the psalm gives its historical background. At the height of his royal power King David looked out from the roof of his palace one spring evening and saw a beautiful woman called Bathsheba bathing on her roof. David lusted after her and committed adultery with her. Wanting to steal her permanently, David arranged for her husband, Uriah the Hittite, to be sent into the most dangerous part of a battle against the Amonnites. As intended, Uriah was killed and David was free to marry Bathsheba. Only when Nathan the prophet was sent by God to confront the newly wedded king did David recognise his guilt, confess his sin and plead for mercy.

These events are recounted in 2 Samuel Chapters 11 and 12. The story ends with David saying: *I have sinned against the Lord* (2 Samuel 12: 13). He later developed his initial confession into this psalm of supplication for God's mercy, cleansing, and renewal. Its words have been immortalised in prayers and liturgies down the centuries. They remain a great source of inspiration to those who seek forgiveness from God with a broken and contrite heart.

The psalm opens with an abject plea for mercy. David is agonising under the dark cloud of his guilty conscience. He offers no excuses and makes no mention of mitigating circumstances. His words, *I know my transgressions and my sin is ever before me* (verse 3), show that he fully understands the gravity and horror of what he has done.

Although David's murder of Uriah was appalling, and although the surrounding sins of adultery, theft and conspiracy were hardly private wrongs, nevertheless the psalm goes to the heart of the matter when it suggests that the worst aspect of the king's evildoing was the magnitude of his sin against God. *Against you, you only, have I sinned* (verse 4).

David had broken the last five of the ten commandments. He knew he was under God's judgement and that he needed God's mercy. He also recognised that his wickedness stemmed from what is called 'original sin' – the inherently sinful nature which all human beings are born with and which makes us all potential rebels against God. The rather puzzling words; *Surely I was sinful at birth, sinful from the time my mother conceived me* (verse 5), do not of course mean that the beautiful processes of conception and birth are sinful. They are a reference to the universal tendency of humanity towards sinfulness or original sin.

Many people remain, throughout their lives, in a state of denial about their own sinfulness. Perhaps we all need a wake-up call to alert us to this fault line in the human character. Feeling conscience-stricken about a serious sin is one way of hearing the wake-up call from God.

David's response was to pray for pardon and purification. He asked to be cleansed, washed, and to have his iniquity blotted out (verses 7–8). Then he prayed; *Create in me a pure heart O God* (verse 10). He wanted the new beginning that only his creator could give him. He pleaded for spiritual renewal making the first reference in the Old Testament to the power of the Holy Spirit (verse 12) several centuries before it was fully revealed in the New Testament.

Up to this point, the tone of the psalm is remorseful and penitential. To this day it is sung to doleful chants in most churches. Yet paradoxically the psalm is also one of gladness and rejoicing (verse 8). Before we reach the end we enter the realm of joy (verse 12), praise (verse 15), and the potential happiness of serving God as a teacher (verse 13).

The greatness of this psalm lies in the beautiful language of penitence with which it tracks David's spiritual journey from the deep mineshaft of guilt to the high mountain of salvation. Many of the Davidic poems devote verses to blaming enemies or rivals. This one is unique in its introspective intimacy before God and in its haunting words of unconditional remorse.

As 21st century readers of the psalm we can discern its voice of inner conscience reaching out in prayer to God who responds by giving inner transformation to the *broken and contrite heart* (verse 17). Those who feel under pressure from the burden of their own guilt are recommended to make a similar journey following in King David's footsteps.

ADDITIONAL NOTES

Form and Title: There is little reason to doubt that this psalm was personally written by David in the aftermath of being confronted by Nathan the prophet. The title may have been added later, but the psalm is too individual to allow room for debate about other authors. It is the best known of the penitential psalms.

Verse 2: *wash away* (see also verse 7): The Hebrew verb suggests the scrubbing of a dirty garment in a laundry.

Cleanse (see also verse 7): The Hebrew verb used in the Levitical rituals for declaring a skin-disease sufferer clean (see Leviticus 13: 6 and 34).

Verses 3–4: The three separate Hebrew words used to describe David's offence have established Biblical meanings. Transgression is the crossing of a boundary. Sin is wandering from God's way. Iniquity is the depravity of nature.

Verse 7: *Hyssop* was the caper plant (*Capparis spinosa*), a bright green creeper which grows out of the fissures of rocks in the Sinaitic valleys. Its stalks and branches were used for sprinkling water or blood in Israelite cleansing rituals (see Leviticus 14: 4; Exodus 12: 22). To this day the caper plant is believed to have cleansing properties in some Middle Eastern communities.

Whiter than snow: Symbolises purity. See also Isaiah 1: 18; *Though your sins are like scarlet they shall be as white as snow*.

Verse 8: *Let the bones you have crushed rejoice*: Several Biblical versions translate the last word more felicitously as 'dance'.

Verse 10: *Create*: A verb used to denote transformation. See Paul's new creation (2 Corinthians 5: 17).

Verse 11: *Holy Spirit*: This theological concept fully revealed in the New Testament is only mentioned twice in the entire Old Testament. Here in this psalm and in Isaiah 63: 10–11.

Verses 16–17: These verses are not a repudiation of sacrifice or its modern equivalent penance. But they are an indication that such activities are acceptable to God only if the penitent's attitude is right, i.e. if it includes a broken and contrite heart.

The psalm as a whole: This is renowned for its 'profound appropriateness as the voice of the penitent soul in all ages.' (12) It is recited on the Day of Atonement in Jewish rituals and on Ash Wednesday in Christian liturgies.

A strange story is told about the psalm's effect on Voltaire who attempted to parody it. Having composed several profane stanzas he reached verse 10; *Create in me a pure heart O God*. At this point Voltaire was so overcome by the psalm's power that he broke down in tears, abandoned his parody, and turned to God in pentinence.

PERSONAL COMMENT

Although my crime (lying on oath about a hotel bill) was not in the same league as David's, I can identify with his guilt feelings. For I, too, had sinned primarily against God by breaking the eighth commandment as well as against my family and my friends by letting them down through my deceit. So I was hit by huge waves of remorse.

A few days after I had been publicly exposed for my lie, an unknown pastor found me sitting on my own for hours in a church in New York. I gave him a garbled version of my troubles. He prayed with me and suggested I should read Psalm 51. When I studied its poignant verses it set me off on a voyage of penitence using the words of the psalm as my navigation points. In the early part of the voyage the waves seemed unbearably rough but by their painful batterings they began the washing and cleansing process.

David does not say in this psalm how long the penitence process took in his case. From certain clues in 2 Samuel 12 it seems as though his crushed bones and broken heart did not mend for several months. The timing was similar for me. A true penitent must not expect instant salvation.

Although my voyage was long and testing, towards the end of it I began to experience the joy of penitence. This sounds a most improbable oxymoron, but like the psalmist I gradually started to hear sounds of *joy and gladness* (verse 8) and my crushed bones did begin to heal and rejoice as I realised that the Holy Spirit was restoring to me the *joy of salvation* (verses 12). So this Jonathan feels a bond with David the author of Psalm 51. From a broken and contrite heart to the joy of God's salvation is a momentous journey. Across the generations it has been made by countless other people under pressure from guilt who have found this psalm a beacon of hope as they seek God's mercy in penitence and faith.

A PRAYER BASED ON PSALM 51

O Lord have mercy upon me, have mercy upon me. For I know I have done wrong. I know that I have sinned against you. I know I have done evil in your sight. I am truly sorry. In penitence I humbly offer you my broken and contrite heart. Please forgive me, cleanse me and wash away my sins.

O God renew me with a pure and clean heart. Please do not turn away from me or withdraw your Holy Spirit from me. Restore your unfailing love to me so that I may be granted the joy of your salvation. Then I will sing your praises and help other sinners to return to you. Through Jesus Christ our Lord. Amen.

PSALM 23: Confidence in God

A psalm of David.

The Lord is my shepherd, I shall not be in want.
   [2] He makes me lie down in green pastures,
he leads me beside quiet waters,
   [3] he restores my soul.
He guides me in paths of righteousness
   for his name's sake.
[4] Even though I walk
   through the valley of the shadow of death,
I will fear no evil,
   for you are with me;
your rod and your staff,
   they comfort me.

[5] You prepare a table before me
   in the presence of my enemies.
You anoint my head with oil;
   my cup overflows.
[6] Surely goodness and love will follow me
   all the days of my life,
and I will dwell in the house of the Lord
   for ever.

REFLECTION

This most loved of psalms has a simple message for people under pressure: Have confidence in God.

To express the power and beauty of his own trusting relationship with God the psalmist uses two metaphors. The shepherd caring for his sheep (verses 1–4) and the host preparing a banquet for his guest (verses 5–6). God is at the centre of both situations. This is made clear by the confident declarations: *The Lord is my shepherd* and *You prepare a table before me* (Verses 1 and 5).

The shepherd part of the psalm evokes idyllic images of sheep lying down in green pastures beside quiet waters. Then comes a reminder that the human flock needs to be morally guided along *paths of righteousness* when searching for the spiritual renewal implied by the phrase *he restores my soul* (verse 3). Jesus used a paraphrased quotation from this psalm, which would have been familiar to his audiences, when he said: *I am the good shepherd* (John 10: 11).

Even when accompanied by the good shepherd, any journey of the soul inevitably passes through dark valleys and ultimately must face death. Few sentences in all scripture have given greater comfort than verse 4: *Even though I walk through the valley of the shadow of death I will fear no evil for you are with me*. It is the last five words, *for you are with me*, that speak so clearly about the reassurance that flows from a personal relationship with the Lord.

In the last two verses of the psalm the scene changes from outdoors to indoors. The imagery is that of the bountiful hospitality of the banqueting hall, but the underlying message again emphasises the individual's special relationship with God the generous host.

The reference to the banquet taking place in the presence of enemies (verse 5) is difficult to interpret. In the royal court of King David captives from the battlefield were sometimes made to attend Israelite victory feasts, but to the contemporary ear this sounds too much like gloating. Perhaps a safer modern parallel might be that of a faithful believer, who has endured past torments at the hands of enemies and is now able to look back on those afflictions with confidence that his relationship with God protected him in the darkest valleys.

The last verse rises to a note of even higher confidence as the psalmist proclaims his joyful certainty that he will dwell in the house of the Lord for ever. Both as a poem and as a message about individual trust in God's provision and protection, Psalm 23 is matchless in its beauty.

ADDITIONAL NOTES

Title: *of David*: Here the superscription may denote the King's personal authorship. This is because of the reference to a royal anointing at the banquet in verse 5.

Verse 4: *Shadow of death*: The literal translation of the Hebrew word *sālmawet* which occurs some twenty times in the Old Testament, e.g., Job 10: 21–22 and 38: 17. It is a much better rendering than the term 'deep darkness' which is used in some versions of the Bible.

Rod and staff: Shepherds in ancient Israel usually carried two implements. A club or rod to drive away wild or human predators and a crook or staff to control the sheep.

Verse 6: *the house of the Lord*: May have been a specific reference to the temple for the Israelites. But Christians, knowing more about life after death from the New Testament, may apply the term to heaven.

PERSONAL COMMENT

While studying theology at Oxford my tutor was Canon Michael Green, a great evangelist, scholar and servant of the Lord. One night in November 2001 Michael began to feel acute pains in his chest. He was rushed by ambulance to the Radcliffe Infirmary in the small hours of the morning. As he lay under arc lights 'on the slab' of the emergency unit with the cardiac team giving him injections, defibrillations, and other treatments the cardiologist told him he had definitely suffered a heart attack.

When I visited Michael on the ward the following day, he described his feelings as he heard this news. 'I thought to myself "Green this could be it!",' he said. 'For as I gazed up into those bright lights above my head it dawned on me that I really was walking through the valley of the shadow of death. Then I was suddenly filled with a wonderful warm glow of joy and peacefulness. I had no fear at all. For I knew the Lord was with me.' (8).

Michael's spiritual confidence under acute physical pressure struck me as a perfect example of Psalm 23's message to the faithful sheep or servant under the shadow of death.

Although he was more than ready to meet his maker, Michael Green made a full recovery. Happily he was able to share in a much more joyful interpretation of the psalm when it was sung at my wedding to Elizabeth on 25 June 2003.

We were married at St Matthews, Westminster, and the church was surrounded by a throng of paparazzi. A few years earlier at the height of my political dramas those press photographers symbolised 'enemies', because they were forever besieging our family home, intruding, chasing, pushing and sometimes literally fighting to get 'today's picture of the beleagured Minister'. Now as the last verse of Psalm 23 soared to the rafters of the church with the high C's of the Crimond descant making the welkin ring, my cup was surely overflowing with goodness and love before the altar table. It was all happening, more or less in the presence of my former 'enemies' from the paparazzi, on this day a most friendly and familiar collection of genial faces. They were simply doing their job just as they had done it in my Ministerial days. It was my attitude and spirit that had been completely transformed. By whom? By the Good Shepherd whom I constantly thank for restoring my soul and guiding this wayward sheep through many dark valleys to the house of the Lord.

A PRAYER BASED ON PSALM 23

Lord, you are my good shepherd. I pray that you will guide me in paths of righteousness and restore my soul. When the time comes for me to walk through the valley of the shadow of death I pray that you will be with me, giving me your protection and comfort. May my cup overflow with your goodness and love all the days of my life as I pray that I will dwell in your house for ever and ever. Amen.

PSALM 73: Pressure from envy

A psalm of Asaph.

Surely God is good to Israel,
  to those who are pure in heart.

[2] But as for me, my feet had almost slipped;
  I had nearly lost my foothold.
[3] For I envied the arrogant
  when I saw the prosperity of the wicked.

[4] They have no struggles;
  their bodies are healthy and strong.
[5] They are free from the burdens common to man;
  they are not plagued by human ills.
[6] Therefore pride is their necklace;
  they clothe themselves with violence.
[7] From their callous hearts comes iniquity;
  the evil conceits of their minds know no limits.
[8] They scoff, and speak with malice;
  in their arrogance they threaten oppression.
[9] Their mouths lay claim to heaven,
  and their tongues take possession of the earth.
[10] Therefore their people turn to them
  and drink up waters in abundance.
[11] They say, 'How can God know?
  Does the Most High have knowledge?'

[12] This is what the wicked are like –
  always carefree, they increase in wealth.

[13] Surely in vain have I kept my heart pure;
  in vain have I washed my hands in innocence.
[14] All day long I have been plagued;
  I have been punished every morning.
[15] If I had said, 'I will speak thus,'
  I would have betrayed your children.

[16] When I tried to understand all this,
    it was oppressive to me
[17] till I entered the sanctuary of God;
    then I understood their final destiny.

[18] Surely you place them on slippery ground;
    you cast them down to ruin.
[19] How suddenly are they destroyed,
    completely swept away by terrors!
[20] As a dream when one awakes,
    so when you arise, O Lord,
    you will despise them as fantasies.

[21] When my heart was grieved
    and my spirit embittered,
[22] I was senseless and ignorant;
    I was a brute beast before you.

[23] Yet I am always with you;
    you hold me by my right hand.
[24] You guide me with your counsel,
    and afterwards you will take me into glory.
[25] Whom have I in heaven but you?
    And earth has nothing I desire besides you.
[26] My flesh and my heart may fail,
    but God is the strength of my heart
    and my portion for ever.

[27] Those who are far from you will perish;
    you destroy all who are unfaithful to you.
[28] But as for me, it is good to be near God.
    I have made the Sovereign Lord my refuge;
    I will tell of all your deeds.

REFLECTION

Envy and bitterness can put people who suffer from these corrosive emotions under heavy pressure. They nearly destroyed the author of this psalm. But after wrestling with his good and bad feelings, which included anxieties about the fairness of God, he found the solution that takes off the pressure and gives inner peace.

The psalm opens with an impeccable declaration of the author's faith: *Surely God is good... to those who are pure in heart* (verse 1). He is referring to himself, a decent and upright man with a belief in God. But then – whoops! – he slips into a negative mindset of envy (verse 3). He delivers an angry rant against the people he loves to hate. He sees them as prosperous and arrogant (verse 3); healthy, strong, and above the worries of ordinary men and women (verses 4–5); so conceited as a result of their worldly success and popularity that they ignore God (verses 9–11); above all, they are wealthy and wicked (verse 12) which the author seems to think are synonymous conditions.

After composing this caricature of his *bêtes noires* the psalmist sinks into self-pity. The phrase; *In vain I have kept myself pure* (verse 13) is a pathetic whinge, equivalent to, 'So what's been in it for me?' However, this expression of his resentment checks him. He starts a process of God-centred self-examination which leads to an understanding of what has been wrongly filling his heart with bitterness (verse 21). Gradually his mood changes as he sees the answer to his challenge.

The mood change starts when the psalmist says *I entered the sanctuary of God; then I understood...* (verse 17). We are not told what was meant by the phrase *entered the sanctuary*. In ancient Israel it involved going into the temple. In the modern world it means having a personal experience of God. Individual believers will relate this to their own spiritual journeys. It may come through prayer, through worship, through teaching or through a conversion. Whatever the process, life starts to look different after such an experience. The psalmist's surprised exclamation *Then I understood* (verse 17) is, in contemporary language, 'Oh, now I get it'.

But what did the psalmist understand and what should we be getting? Many people in the early stages of their spiritual journey become perplexed by age-old questions such as, 'Why do the wicked prosper?', or, 'Why doesn't my virtue bring its reward?' There are honest doubts about the value of staying faithful in an unfaithful world. This psalm teaches us that watching the worldly and the wicked with envy is a short-sighted activity. So is gazing at our own navels with self-pity. We have to look upwards to God and try to see things as he sees them.

God's vision is completely different. We human creatures of earthly time have great difficulty in getting our heads round his heavenly eternity. But the psalmist managed it. After he had entered the sanctuary of God he saw that his hate figures were *on slippery ground* (verse 18). They were heading for a different final destiny of ruin, terror and destruction (verses 18–19). By contrast the believer trusts in God's promise; *I am always with you* (verse 24). Then in one of the most beautiful proclamations of personal faith in the Old Testament he declares: *Whom have I in heaven but you? And earth has nothing I desire beside you* (verse 25). His final judgement on this puzzling conundrum of why the ungodly prosper while the godly struggle is: *Those who are far from you will perish … but as for me it is good to be near God* (verses 27–28).

The psalmist's personal testimony has a wide contemporary relevance. Competition in today's rat race puts many people under pressure to keep up with the Jones'. Most of us have our moments of wanting to be strong, proud, healthy, beautiful, powerful and rich. These obsessions tend to squeeze out God. Those who are captivated by them are often the ungodly, sometimes, the wicked. Yet on the surface they succeed and prosper. So it is logical for the less successful believer to ask the same question that the psalmist asked; Why has life treated me unfairly?

The answer to this question is not to be found in logic, in materialism, nor even in the present time. Only after reaching the crossroads of verse 17 can we understand that the joy of communion with God transcends temporal values and brings its ultimate rewards in eternal life.

ADDITIONAL NOTES

Title and form: *A psalm of Asaph*: This is the first of the eleven psalms of Asaph, a director of the temple choir in the reign of David. It is a psalm of personal testimony. Scholars are divided on whether it should be categorised as a lament psalm, a thanksgiving psalm or a wisdom psalm. B. W. Anderson calls it 'the greatest of the wisdom psalms' (9), a judgement many will agree with because its wisdom still seems so relevant today.

Verse 1: *to Israel*: Means in its wider context God's faithful people.

Verse 6: *Pride is their necklace*: In ancient Israel a necklace symbolised power and pride. See Genesis 41: 42 when Pharaoh put a gold necklace on Joseph after giving him control of Egypt. See also Isaiah 3: 16–18 when the haughty women of Jerusalem with their outstretched necks are condemned for their 'crescent necklaces' and other finery.

Verse 13: *In vain have I washed my hands in innocence* is a bitter expression of regret for all the time the psalmist has spent washing his hands in purification rituals.

Verse 17: *the sanctuary of God*: Probably the inner courts of the temple but see Reflection (page 39) for a contemporary meaning.

Verse 18: *on slippery ground*: Of Deuteronomy 32: 35 – 'in due time their foot will slip'.

Verse 23: Derek Kidner makes a valuable point about the Hebrew tenses here. They are: God has held, he does guide, he will glorify his servant. It is a steady progression (15).

Comment on the psalm as a whole: 'This psalm is an act of faith. It is a mighty engagement with God, a struggle against God and a wondrous communion with God.' (Walter Breuegemann, *The Message of the Psalms*.)

PERSONAL COMMENT

My feet slipped. No 'almost' about it (verse 2). When I was a keen competitor in the worlds of politics, power, business and celebrity I forgot about God for most of the time and my life bore plenty of resemblance to that of the arrogant and wealthy characters described in verses 3–12.

When you're in the middle of the rat race it's easy to feel envious of those ahead of you. On the whole this wasn't my problem. I don't quite know why. Maybe I thought I was out in front in the race. Maybe I inherited an envy-free disposition from my good-natured father. But I certainly became aware of other people's envy towards me, including the envy of outwardly devout Christians. Perhaps they thought to themselves, 'why does that wicked man prosper?' I don't blame them, although now I know that they must have been a long way from *entering the sanctuary* of verse 17.

I love this psalm because it is such an honest wrestling match between the believing, envious and doubting aspects of the author's character. It is an authentic struggle for Godly faith in an ungodly world. I hope and pray that I have resolved that struggle in my own life. But should envy and bitterness ever start to torment me, I would go back and study Psalm 73. I hope its verses would persuade me that there is nothing in heaven or in earth worth desiring more than a relationship with the Lord. I hope I could then say: *As for me, it is good to be near God* (verse 28).

A PRAYER BASED ON PSALM 73

O Lord, I am trying to be a good follower of your ways but I know I am slipping. I can't help feeling envious of those arrogant and successful people who take no notice of you and even mock you. Yet they go from strength to strength while I remain weak and unsuccessful in life's races. Have I been wasting my time following you and believing in you?

Lord forgive me for asking such a question. For you have shown me the answer. I have been in your presence and now I understand. Those people I used to envy are heading to a different destination. You have held me by the hand. You are guiding me. You will take me into your glory. I want nothing else than to be with you in heaven and in earth. For it is good for me to be near to God. Amen.

PSALM 139: Who is God?

For the director of music. Of David. A psalm.

O Lord, you have searched me
   and you know me.
[2] You know when I sit and when I rise;
   you perceive my thoughts from afar.
[3] You discern my going out and my lying down;
   you are familiar with all my ways.
[4] Before a word is on my tongue
   you know it completely, O Lord.

[5] You hem me in – behind and before;
   you have laid your hand upon me.
[6] Such knowledge is too wonderful for me,
   too lofty for me to attain.

[7] Where can I go from your Spirit?
   Where can I flee from your presence?
[8] If I go up to the heavens, you are there;
   if I make my bed in the depths, you are there.
[9] If I rise on the wings of the dawn,
   if I settle on the far side of the sea,
[10] even there your hand will guide me,
   your right hand will hold me fast.

[11] If I say, 'Surely the darkness will hide me
   and the light become night around me,'
[12] even the darkness will not be dark to you;
   the night will shine like the day,
   for darkness is as light to you.

[13] For you created my inmost being;
   you knit me together in my mother's womb.
[14] I praise you because I am fearfully and wonderfully made;
   your works are wonderful,
   I know that full well.
[15] My frame was not hidden from you
   when I was made in the secret place.

When I was woven together in the depths of the earth,
   [16] your eyes saw my unformed body.
All the days ordained for me
   were written in your book
   before one of them came to be.

[17] How precious to me are your thoughts, O God!
   How vast is the sum of them!
[18] Were I to count them,
   they would outnumber the grains of sand.
When I awake,
   I am still with you.

[19] If only you would slay the wicked, O God!
   Away from me, you bloodthirsty men!
[20] They speak of you with evil intent;
   your adversaries misuse your name.
[21] Do I not hate those who hate you, O Lord,
   and abhor those who rise up against you?
[22] I have nothing but hatred for them;
   I count them my enemies.

[23] Search me, O God, and know my heart;
   test me and know my anxious thoughts.
[24] See if there is any offensive way in me,
   *and lead me in the way everlasting.

REFLECTION

All the previous nine psalms have in one way or another offered hope to the people under pressure by appealing to God. Perhaps we should pause to see whether there is a psalm which can help us to answer one of the most searching questions of all time: Who is God?

Psalm 139 is a great and glorious psalm which responds to the question perhaps more beautifully and more deeply than any other passage in the Old Testament. The psalmist gives his answer in sublime poetry which is both intimate and universal in its appeal. On the one hand this is a personal account of the author's understanding of the God he has come to know and love. Yet on the other hand it expresses thoughts of such soaring grandeur that they have illuminated the nature of God to human hearts across centuries and civilisations. No wonder Psalm 139 is often called 'the crown of psalms'.

The jewel in the crown is the author's relationship with God. Although he writes about it in a narrative that falls into sections which can be classified under high faluting headings such as: God's omniscience; God's omnipresence; God's omnipotence and so on, nevertheless one should never lose sight of the fact that this psalm is a personal testimony. It begins at a point in the author's spiritual journey when in fear and trembling he realises that God has searched him out and known him. It ends with the confident and joyful cry: *Search me O God and know my heart, test me...* From that fear to that confidence is a momentous advance in human understanding of the divine nature. To take others along the same road it is best to stay in the company of the psalmist as he tells his story in four parts which can be headed:

How God knows me
How God stays close to me
How God made me
How God tests me

How God knows me (verses 1–6)
The first six verses are written in a tone of anxiety, if not fear.

The author uses a succession of scrutinising verbs to illustrate the in-depth nature of God's investigation. He *searches, knows, perceives, discerns* and is *familiar with* every aspect of the individual's life (verses 1–3). God does it all *from afar* (verse 2), a phrase which almost suggests surveillance by celestial CCTV cameras. Next comes celestial telepathy for God taps into the psalmist's thoughts and knows what he is going to say before he says it. This is all too much for the author to bear. He feels hemmed in (verse 5) and his mind turns to ways of escape.

Transferring these thoughts from the personal to the general, we all need to face up to the fact that nothing can be hidden from an all-seeing all-knowing God. Archbishop Cranmer summarised this as well as anyone in the opening line of his great collect: 'Almighty God unto whom all hearts be open and from whom no secrets are hid'. We may reject God if we choose to do so but we cannot escape from him.

How God stays close to me (Verses 7–12)

This part of the psalm is written in awe and gratitude. The psalmist answers his own rhetorical questions about fleeing from God's spirit in verses of unsurpassed beauty.

> *If I rise on the wings of the dawn*
> *if I settle on the far side of the sea*
> *even here your hand will guide me*
> *your right hand will hold me fast* (verses 9–10)

By now the tone has changed from fear to joy at the discovery that hiding from God is impossible. Like many people in primitive society the psalmist may have feared the hours of darkness but now he is realising the blessings of divine companionship in them as he writes: *even the darkness will not be dark to you ... for darkness is as light to you* (verse 12).

The verses in this part of the psalm are well-known and much quoted. They have inspired countless musicians, artists and writers. Perhaps the most famous poem to derive from the psalmist's words is Francis Thompson's *The Hound of Heaven*. But the appeal of the original Hebrew poetry itself is universal and speaks more powerfully than any other voice.

How God made me (Verses 13–18)

God searches us out not only because he knows us but because he made us. The psalmist delves into the mysteries of childbirth, genetics, and the pre-natal life of a foetus in the mother's womb to develop his theme. Since he had no scientific knowledge of these mysteries, the depth of his understanding of them is all the more impressive, once again expressed in exquisitely beautiful poetry. The key line here is: *I praise you because I am fearfully and wonderfully made* (verse 14). All the glory is given to our sovereign Lord and Creator. Not only did this amazing creator-God make us; from conception to death he plans our lives with incredible care and detail. This divine knowledge sends the psalmist into rapture as he praises God for his vast and precious thoughts about each individual human being. If they could be counted *they would outnumber the grains of sand* (verse 14). The last verse in this section; *When I awake I am still with you* (verse 15) is uncertain in meaning, but probably refers to awakening from the sleep of death into a new life with God in heaven.

How God treats me (verses 19–24)

This final part of the psalm opens on what seems to be an angry and discordant note after so much poetic beauty. *Away with you, you bloodthirsty men* (verse 19) cries the author as he appeals to God to slay the wicked.

Yet as John Stott and other eminent commentators have pointed out, what seems jarring to modern ears would have been natural to the ears of ancient Israel. The psalmist is full of that robust Old Testament virtue – righteous indignation. He is not expressing feelings of revenge or personal animosity. He is abominating what we in the 21st century sometimes too easily tolerate – those who mock God, hate his laws, and do evil in his sight. So the author is simply proclaiming his willingness to fight the good fight on God's side.

Secure in the knowledge that God knows him and watches over him, the psalmist has become confident enough in the relationship to welcome divine testing of his character and way of life. So he rounds off the psalm with an admission that he does have some anxieties about his own sinful nature. To tackle this problem head on, in the final verses he issues an invitation with joyful confidence:

> *Search me O God and know my heart*
> *test me and know my anxious thoughts.*

This makes a sharp contrast with the faltering tone of verse 1 when the psalmist was fearful about being searched. Now he can't have enough of it! The purpose of his invitation is to be cleansed from sin so that God can lead him in the *way everlasting* (verse 24).

The psalm as a whole takes us on a journey of spiritual discovery by a great poet. His words are a wonderful inspiration to all who seek to understand the nature of God.

ADDITIONAL NOTES

Form and title: This psalm is individual but defies all other classification. It stands alone.

Of David: The authorship is open but some scholars have detected Aramaic expressions in the language which they think makes it unlikely to have been written by David himself.

Verse 2: *sit down and rise*: A Hebrew expression meaning whatever I do in every aspect of my life.

Verse 5: *hem me in*: The verb in Hebrew carries pejorative connotations. Elsewhere in the Old Testament it is often translated as 'besieging'.

Verse 8: *in the depths*: Means Sheol, the Hebrew pit of death into which God was thought never to go. See Psalm 88: 5. The inconsistency is unimportant. This psalmist clearly meant to say that God accompanied him everywhere even in Sheol.

Verse 9: *wings of the dawn*: Means in the east and *far side of the sea* means in the west (*cf.* Amos 9: 2–4). So the psalmist was using the analogy of a journey from farthest east to farthest west, but God was still with him.

Verse 14: The phrase *fearfully and wonderfully made* was first composed by the *Book of Common Prayer* translator Miles Coverdale. Scholars argue about its fidelity but it certainly captures the spirit of these verses which is presumably why the NIV translation has accepted it.

Verse 15: *made in the secret place*: Means conceived in the womb.

Verse 18: *When I awake*: See Reflection.

Verses 13–18: Michael Wilcock comments: 'Not just from birth to death but from conception to death a human life is God's handiwork. Psalm 139 is his forthright "No" to those who for reasons of their own would cut it off by abortion at one end or by euthanasia at the other.' (11).

Verse 24: *the way everlasting*: Meaning the way of eternity, the ancient way (*cf.* Jeremiah 6: 16) which God taught from the beginning and which endures for ever in contrast to the way of the wicked which will perish (see Psalm 1: 6).

PERSONAL COMMENT

This is my favourite psalm in the entire psalter. It took time to appreciate its beautiful poetry but eventually it gave me an understanding of God far beyond the range of my normal imagination.

Greater minds than mine have stumbled before being introduced to Psalm 139. 'Erasmus your thoughts on God are too human', (12) said Martin Luther to his fellow 16th century theologian as they embarked together on a joint study of this psalm.

The humanity of the psalmist is something I find particularly attractive. Although he was clearly inspired to poetic genius by his thoughts of God, at the beginning of the psalm he comes across as a simple and rather vulnerable person. In the first verse he is self-defensive and fearful about being searched by God. But by the last verse he has been transformed into a confident self-improver ready to accept any amount of divine searchings.

Although only a struggling self-improver I love this psalm and use two verses of it every morning in my daily quiet time. I got started on this habit in prison. This was thanks to a friend from Jersey, Peter Cushen, who sent me in a present of C. H. Spurgeon's three volume commentary of the psalms *The Treasury of David*. It is a book I warmly recommend, although only to those with a taste for gargantuan Victorian Biblical commentaries.

In *The Treasury of David*, after each psalm has been exhaustively analysed by the author, an additional page or two is given over to 'Quaint Sayings' – i.e., comments by experts other than Spurgeon. Towards the end of the quaint sayings on psalm 139 there is a quotation from *Homiletic Commentary* by T. Wallace suggesting that verses 23 and 24 should be used as 'a beautiful and impressive prayer for the commencement of each day. It is also a great sentiment to admonish us at the beginning of each day' (13).

I took this suggestion on board and found it worked wonders. *Search me O God and know my heart* is a perfect opening to prayers of confession. *Lead me in the way everlasting* is a splendid conclusion to prayers for a start to the new day. I recommend T. Wallace's advice and of course the whole psalm to other searched and searching people under pressure.

A PRAYER BASED ON PSALM 139

O Lord you have searched me out and known me. You know everything about me – what was, and is, and is to come in my life. For you are an all knowing, all seeing, all powerful and ever present God. Your thoughts about me are too vast, too numerous, and too wonderful to understand, yet I know that I am yours and that you are watching ceaselessly over me.

So search me O God and know my heart. Test me and know my thoughts. See if there are any offending ways in me. Then cleanse me and lead me in your way everlasting. Through Jesus Christ Our Lord. Amen.

PART II

SPECIAL SITUATIONS OF PRESSURE

PSALM 22: Agonising pressure

For the director of music. To (the tune of)
'The Doe of the Morning'. A psalm of David.

My God, my God, why have you forsaken me?
  Why are you so far from saving me,
    so far from the words of my groaning?
[2] O my God, I cry out by day, but you do not answer,
  by night, and am not silent.

[3] Yet you are enthroned as the Holy One;
  you are the praise of Israel.
[4] In you our fathers put their trust;
  they trusted and you delivered them.
[5] They cried to you and were saved;
  in you they trusted and were not disappointed.

[6] But I am a worm and not a man,
  scorned by men and despised by the people.
[7] All who see me mock me;
  they hurl insults, shaking their heads:
[8] 'He trusts in the Lord;
  let the Lord rescue him.
Let him deliver him,
  since he delights in him.'

[9] Yet you brought me out of the womb;
  you made me trust in you
    even at my mother's breast.
[10] From birth I was cast upon you;
  from my mother's womb you have been my God.
[11] Do not be far from me,
  for trouble is near
    and there is no-one to help.

[12] Many bulls surround me;
  strong bulls of Bashan encircle me.

[13] Roaring lions tearing their prey
    open their mouths wide against me.
[14] I am poured out like water,
    and all my bones are out of joint.
My heart has turned to wax;
    it has melted away within me.
[15] My strength is dried up like a potsherd,
    and my tongue sticks to the roof of my mouth;
    you lay me in the dust of death.
[16] Dogs have surrounded me;
    a band of evil men has encircled me,
    they have pierced my hands and my feet.

[17] I can count all my bones;
    people stare and gloat over me.
[18] They divide my garments among them
    and cast lots for my clothing.
[19] But you, O Lord, be not far off;
    O my Strength, come quickly to help me.
[20] Deliver my life from the sword,
    my precious life from the power of the dogs.
[21] Rescue me from the mouth of the lions;   *The doe or hind surrounded.*
    save me from the horns of the wild oxen.

[22] I will declare your name to my brothers;
    in the congregation I will praise you.
[23] You who fear the Lord, praise him!
    All you descendants of Jacob, honour him!
    Revere him, all you descendants of Israel!
[24] For he has not despised or disdained
    the suffering of the afflicted one;
he has not hidden his face from him
    but has listened to his cry for help.

[25] From you comes the theme of my praise in the great
        assembly;
    before those who fear you will I fulfil my vows.

[26] The poor will eat and be satisfied;
 they who seek the Lord will praise him –
 may your hearts live for ever!

[27] All the ends of the earth
 will remember and turn to the Lord,
and all the families of the nations
 will bow down before him,
[28] for dominion belongs to the Lord
 and he rules over the nations.

[29] All the rich of the earth will feast and worship;
 all who go down to the dust will kneel before him –
 those who cannot keep themselves alive.
[30] Posterity will serve him;
 future generations will be told about the Lord.
[31] They will proclaim his righteousness
 to a people yet unborn –
 for he has done it.

REFLECTION

This extraordinary psalm combines agonising cries of pain with amazing words of prophecy. No Christian believer can read it without bringing to mind the horrors of the crucifixion. Yet it is an historical fact that the psalm was written many hundreds of years before the scenes of the cross, so uncannily depicted in these verses, actually took place. So there is a mystery here. It is a mystery with a message for people under pressure.

The psalm opens with the haunting words *My God, my God, why have you forsaken me* (verse 1). The identical cry came from the lips of Jesus in his death agony on the cross. Was he quoting the psalm? Many Christians have been persuaded to accept this view but the notion is surely implausible. When a man is being executed he does not reach for the *Oxford Dictionary of Quotations*. The idea of Jesus behaving in an equivalent way on the cross seems just as fanciful. As the commentator Michael Wilcox has written: 'Only those with no feeling for the *mot juste* would speak of our Lord's "quoting" or even "using" these words at such a moment of agony. They were as genuinely his own as they had been the psalmists. But the fact is that we do find them on the lips of both.' (14)

The facts become even stranger. The psalm is a poetic portrait of a man going through the worst ordeals of physical torture and emotional trauma during a humiliating public punishment – possibly the preliminary stages of an execution. He is mocked and insulted (verse 7). He hears the taunts of the crowd shaking their heads in mockery and saying: *He trusts in the Lord, let the Lord rescue him* (verse 8). His sufferings include a terrible thirst, pain from disjointed bones, and agony from the piercing of his hands and feet. His clothes were shared out by the casting of lots (verse 8). As these actual scenes were all played out at Jesus' crucifixion, it is easy to understand why Christian tradition regards Psalm 22 as a prophecy.

The author not only wrote this psalm with the voice of a prophet, he also spoke with the voice of experience. The first 21 verses are too deep a cry of anguish to have been composed from imagination. Yet what is really extraordinary are not the details of the sufferer's pain but his spiritual agony over his God forsaken-ness. This is an experience many others have shared. 'Where is God when we really need him?' is not merely the title of a Philip Yancey best seller, but also a familiar complaint. Yet the sufferer in this psalm is not a despairing complainer. He is bewildered by God's silence but he does not lose his faith in God's presence. Even when surrounded by evil men who he compares with bulls, lions, dogs and wild oxen, he keeps on appealing to the Lord to come quickly and save him (verses 19–21).

The last ten verses of the psalm are a sudden and dramatic change of tone, from agony to ecstasy. We are not told how God rescued his suffering servant. All we learn is that the Lord did not *disdain the afflicted one* but *listened to his cry for help* (verse 24).

In the final verse the psalm swells into an anthem of glory and more prophecy as it predicts that all over the world God's message will be proclaimed to *people yet unborn* (verse 31) and that all the ends of the earth will ... *turn to the Lord* (verse 27).

People under pressure can take heart from this psalm. However dire their circumstances may be and however perplexing the divine silences can seem, God is faithful. In this life or the next, the Lord will raise up his suffering servants and give them his glory, just as he did with the author of this psalm and with his crucified Son.

ADDITIONAL NOTES

Title and Form: *The Doe of the Morning* (also translated as 'The Hind of the Dawn'): This musical instruction may be a way of highlighting the author's theme. For the doe, or hind, is the most gentle of animals symbolising the suffering innocence of the victim in the psalm who is surrounded by bulls, dogs, lions and wild oxen.

This is an individual lament psalm, often known as 'The Psalm of the Cross'.

Verse 1: The opening words were said by Jesus from the cross in Aramaic: *Eloi, Eloi, lama sabacthani* (see Matthew 27: 46; Mark 15: 34).

Verses 7–8: The mockery of these verses and even the taunts of *He trusts in the Lord ... Let him deliver him* are strongly echoed in the Gospel passion narratives (see Matthew 27: 39–44; Mark 15: 31–32; Luke 23: 35).

Verse 12: Bulls of Bashan came from a region of rich pasture grazing in northern Transjordan famous for producing fat cows and strong bulls (see Deuteronomy 32: 14 and Amos 4: 1).

Verses 12–18: Derek Kidner writes: 'This is a scene often enacted: the strong closing in on the weak, the many on the one. The crowd is pictured as bestial (bulls, lions, dogs, wild oxen) but it is all too human whether the deed is done with subtlety or with the brutality of Calvary.'

Verses 14–17: The sufferer's disjointed bones, thirst, and pierced hands and feet are a remarkably accurate description of the horrors of crucifixion although they are not specifically quoted as applying to Jesus in the Gospels.

Verse 18: The division of Jesus' clothes by lot at the foot of the cross by Roman soldiers is described in John 19: 23–24.

PERSONAL COMMENT

No physical torment or punishment that I have ever undergone begins to compare with the agonies suffered by the author of this psalm. However, plenty of similar emotional agony from mocking came my way particularly when the tabloid newspapers first labelled me as a 'Born Again Christian'. The sharpest insults on this score came from a former parliamentary colleague turned columnist and from a newspaper editor who had been my contemporary when we were both young reporters. Their fulminations did not shake my faith. After a while I was even able to get some mild amusement by casting them in the roles of fat bulls of Bashan, roaring lions and wild oxen. There is nothing new in ridiculing a bruised pilgrim, who has to learn to turn the other cheek.

Although the testing period was painful I came to realise that the mockers always fade away whereas God's grace is everlasting. My cries for help in prayer, like the psalmist's, were answered in the end. The pressure faded and a new life dawned. The gospel of salvation is universal.

A PRAYER BASED ON PSALM 22

Lord, Lord, you seem to be so far away from me. Have you forsaken me? I am crying out to you by day and by night in my distress but you do not answer. Why, oh why?

Yet I know you are a great and holy God who does not reject those who trust in you. I am being tormented, mocked and humiliated. Lord, do not leave me to suffer. Rescue me please from my enemies who are like beasts. Save me and deliver me from them. Amen.

PSALM 31: Pressure from all sides

For the director of music. A psalm of David.

In you, O Lord, I have taken refuge;
    let me never be put to shame;
    deliver me in your righteousness.
[2] Turn your ear to me,
    come quickly to my rescue;
be my rock of refuge,
    a strong fortress to save me.
[3] Since you are my rock and my fortress,
    for the sake of your name lead and guide me.
[4] Free me from the trap that is set for me,
    for you are my refuge.
[5] Into your hands I commit my spirit;
    redeem me, O Lord, the God of truth.

[6] I hate those who cling to worthless idols;
    I trust in the Lord.
[7] I will be glad and rejoice in your love,
    for you saw my affliction
    and knew the anguish of my soul.
[8] You have not handed me over to the enemy
    but have set my feet in a spacious place.

[9] Be merciful to me, O Lord, for I am in distress;
    my eyes grow weak with sorrow,
    my soul and my body with grief.
[10] My life is consumed by anguish
    and my years by groaning;
my strength fails because of my affliction,
    and my bones grow weak.
[11] Because of all my enemies,
    I am the utter contempt of my neighbours;
I am a dread to my friends –
    those who see me on the street flee from me.

[12] I am forgotten by them as though I were dead;
  I have become like broken pottery.
[13] For I hear the slander of many;
  there is terror on every side;
they conspire against me
  and plot to take my life.

[14] But I trust in you, O Lord;
  I say, 'You are my God.'
[15] My times are in your hands;
  deliver me from my enemies
  and from those who pursue me.
[16] Let your face shine on your servant;
  save me in your unfailing love.
[17] Let me not be put to shame, O Lord,
  for I have cried out to you;
but let the wicked be put to shame
  and lie silent in the grave.
[18] Let their lying lips be silenced,
  for with pride and contempt
  they speak arrogantly against the righteous.

[19] How great is your goodness,
  which you have stored up for those who fear you,
which you bestow in the sight of men
  on those who take refuge in you.
[20] In the shelter of your presence you hide them
  from the intrigues of men;
in your dwelling you keep them safe
  from accusing tongues.

[21] Praise be to the Lord,
  for he showed his wonderful love to me
  when I was in a besieged city.
[22] In my alarm I said,
  'I am cut off from your sight!'
Yet you heard my cry for mercy
  when I called to you for help.

[23] Love the Lord, all his saints!
   The Lord preserves the faithful,
   but the proud he pays back in full.
[24] Be strong and take heart,
   all you who hope in the Lord.

REFLECTION

Although this psalm opens with a brave declaration of faith (verses 1–8), it soon becomes clear that it is a cry of pain from an author in deep trouble. His woes include physical and mental illness, hostility from friends, slander from enemies, paranoia about plots, and sheer terror. Here indeed is a person under pressure from many directions, but his trust in God helps him to regain his equilibrium.

From verse 9 onwards this psalm whirls downwards into a vortex of despair. The author is sick, getting weaker, and suffering from some form of nervous breakdown for he declares that his whole life is *consumed by anguish* (verse 10). The cause of all this grief is his *affliction*, which in many versions of the Bible is translated more accurately from the original Hebrew as 'guilt' or 'iniquity'. It is clear that something worse than illness must be the root cause of the problem for the psalmist goes on to tell us that he is held in contempt by his friends and neighbours while his enemies are terrorising him with plots and conspiracies. What can he do?

There are many man-made problems in life to which there are no man-made solutions. The author knows this. That is why, when he hits rock bottom he cries out: *Be merciful to me O Lord* (verse 9) which he amplifies with a powerful prayer: *You are my God, my times are in your hands; deliver me from my enemies ... save me in your unfailing love* (verses 14–16).

Whatever the psalmist had done to create his guilt feelings, he also had God-feelings of deep faith and trust. His knowledge of God's mercy and protection provides him with an inner strength. That is why he prays so fervently and evidently so effectively. By the time we reach the end of the psalm the author is praising the Lord for his response to the cry for mercy. That response does not seem to be an ending to the problems but the giving of enough strength to get through them. The *wonderful love* (verse 21) is not a miraculous restoration of the author's health and happiness. It is more like the 'perfect love which casts out fear' (1 John 4: 18). Even in the worst of life's horrors and terrors the faithful believer learns how to cope with the worst pressures. Trusting prayer gives a comfort and an assurance which comes only from true fellowship with God.

ADDITIONAL NOTES

Form and title: The structure and language of this psalm are familiar territory to experienced readers. Many of the phrases in it have been used in earlier psalms (e.g., 4: 6, 6: 2, 6: 7, 28: 2, 30: 4). The ingredients of an appeal for mercy, a response from God, and a concluding doxology of thanks and praise are parts of an established pattern. Yet this familiarity highlights a common experience of God answering the prayers of those in distress.

Verse 5: *Into your hands I commit my spirit*: The words quoted by Jesus in his final saying from the cross (Luke 23: 46).

Verse 6. *worthless idols*: Jonah's prayer (Jonah 2: 8) draws on this verse.

Verse 16: The phrase *terror on every side* was quoted almost obsessively by the prophet Jeremiah in his troubles (see Jeremiah 6: 25; 20: 3; 20: 10; 46: 5; 49: 29).

Verse 23: *His saints*: Means fellow believers who accepted God's covenant.

PERSONAL COMMENT

I can relate to this psalm because of my experiences at the lowest point of my troubles. On 19 January 1999 after much heart searching and conflicting legal advice, I entered a plea of guilty to charges of perjury at London's Central Criminal Court. My plea surprised the media who, freed of all reporting restrictions, savaged me with extreme ferocity. These attacks, coupled with the certainty that I was going to be sentenced to a term of imprisonment a few weeks later, threw me into a state of clinical depression coupled with physical illness. I was bedridden for a week with flu, pneumonia and, worst of all, an occlusion – a mini stroke which burst most of the blood vessels in my left eye, severely impairing my sight.

All these troubles were symptoms of a deeper feeling of guilt – very like the psalmist's. My spiritual reactions were similar to his too. For realising my utter helplessness and total guilt, all I could do was to pray in faith for God's mercy and forgiveness. Again, like the psalmist, I was granted it. That answer to prayer changed nothing in the unpleasant consequences I had to face. It changed everything about the way I faced them. Fear and trembling were gradually replaced by a peaceful acceptance of God's will and a prayerful trust that he would be with me on my prison journey. He was.

A PRAYER BASED ON PSALM 31

Be merciful to me O Lord for I am in pain, distress and anguish. Rejection and humiliation are facing me on every side. I am terrified.

But I trust you O Lord. You are my God. I am in your hands. Save me with your unfailing love. Amen.

PSALM 6: Pressure from illness

For the director of music. With stringed instruments.
According to sheminith. A psalm of David.

O Lord, do not rebuke me in your anger
   or discipline me in your wrath.
[2] Be merciful to me, Lord, for I am faint;
   O Lord, heal me, for my bones are in agony.
[3] My soul is in anguish.
   How long, O Lord, how long?

[4] Turn, O Lord, and deliver me;
   save me because of your unfailing love.
[5] No-one remembers you when he is dead.
   Who praises you from his grave?

[6] I am worn out from groaning;
   all night long I flood my bed with weeping
   and drench my couch with tears.
[7] My eyes grow weak with sorrow;
   they fail because of all my foes.

[8] Away from me, all you who do evil,
   for the Lord has heard my weeping.
[9] The Lord has heard my cry for mercy;
   the Lord accepts my prayer.
[10] All my enemies will be ashamed and dismayed;
   they will turn back in sudden disgrace.

REFLECTION

This psalm is a cry of anguish by an author suffering from severe physical and perhaps nervous illness. With the emotional temperature rising his fear leads him into false nightmares about punishment and death. He is so traumatised that he almost loses heart completely. Yet by the end of the psalm his sobs of depression have been replaced by a surge of confidence.

The pain of the psalmist is graphically described. His bones are in agony, he is worn out from groaning and his eyes are weak from weeping and sorrow (verses 2, 6, 7). No wonder he cries out with a question that all down the ages people under pressure have asked God: 'How long, O Lord, how long?'.

Patience under pressure of physical suffering is perhaps the most difficult of all virtues to achieve. In his impatience the author worries whether he is being punished (verse 1) and heading for oblivion in a forgotten grave (verse 5). Both these anxieties are misplaced for they belong to a pre-Christian era of faith. The concept of sickness as a punishment is totally alien to the New Testament God of Love. So is the concept of death without an after life.

Tossing and turning on his bed of tears the psalmist shudders at the prospect of Sheol, the Hebrew name for the grave (verse 5). Evidently he is terrified of it as a pit of oblivion in which no life or communication can take place. This pessimistic mythology reflects Judaism's view on the finality of death. It was exploded by the resurrection of Jesus Christ who, in the words of St Paul, *has destroyed death and has brought life and immortality to light through the gospel* (2 Timothy 1: 10).

Serious illness can damage our faculties and distort our judgement but it cannot destroy our instinctive desire to pray. This psalm reminds us that sickness may unlock that desire. Negative intimations of our mortality can be positive wake up calls which prompt us into thoughts and prayers about our relationship with God.

In the early verses the psalmist voices three positive and personally addressed prayers to God: *Be merciful to me Lord ... O Lord heal me ... O Lord save me because of your unfailing love* (verses 2–4). These supplications are both physical and spiritual requests as the use of the words *bones* and *soul* in verses 2–3 indicates. There is evidently quite a long pause after the prayers because the psalmist has time to sink into catatonic gloom about his possible demise (verse 5) and to provide much lachrymose detail about his descent into sorrow and weakness (verse 6). Anyone who has had to endure a serious illness will know that such moments of depression can be as real today as they were three thousand years ago.

As we reach the final strophe or stanza of the psalm, depression is replaced with defiance. God is suddenly addressed with vigour in the third person. The latter may have been for liturgical reasons. The most convincing interpretation of the title (see Additional Notes) suggests this psalm could have been a chant in eight parts accompanied by harps and lyres. Whatever the musical explanations, the psychological changes are clear. The Lord has heard the patient's cry for mercy (verse 8) and has transformed him from a groaner into a fighter.

This ultimate revelation of new found confidence, the hallmark of many a psalm of supplication, provides a rousing finale. The line: *Away from me you evil doers* (verse 8) was quoted by Jesus in the sermon on the mount (Matthew 7: 23). It represents a reassertion of power. The patient has regained his strength and put his demons to flight. The psalm as a whole tells us that in sickness or in health God listens to our prayers. He often responds to them by wiping away our tears and rebuilding our confidence.

ADDITIONAL NOTES

Title and form: Sheminith: Means eighth and has musical connotations. See 1 Chronicles 15: 20–21, where eight Levites were instructed to play harps and lyres as they sang 'according to sheminith'.

Of David: Scholars are divided on whether this psalm is personal to King David or generally of the Davidic era. In form this is a psalm of personal lament.

Verse 5: *Sheol,* or the grave: A term that appears frequently in the psalms. The ancient people of Israel feared it as a dark pit or sepulchral cavern which cut the dead off from worshipping God.

Verse 8: *Away with you all you who do evil*: The Norwegian scholar S. G. Mowinckel in his early commentary *Palmenstudien* argued that throughout the psalms 'workers of evil' (16) were sorcerers who cast spells on the sick. Other scholars take a more general view of the phrase.

Jesus quotes verse 8 in Matthew 7: 23.

PERSONAL COMMENT

I have had more serious illness in my life than most people (spending over four years in hospitals and nursing homes) but as the longest of these medical troubles occurred in my childhood, I never suffered from the sort of adult anguish expressed by the psalmist.

There may, however, be another explanation for my lack of anguish. My worst illness was TB in the pre-antibiotic days of the 1940s. By the time it was diagnosed, the infection had spread into both lungs and into my back and hip bones. Eminent specialists were consulted. The optimistic diagnosis was 'this child may live but he will never walk'. The pessimistic diagnosis was 'this child cannot live'. Fortunately there was one dissenter, Dr Macaulay, the senior orthopaedic consultant at Cappagh Hospital in Dublin. He prescribed a three-year period of total immobility strapped to a metal and plaster cast called 'the frame', a primitive precursor of the iron lung.

My years on the frame at Cappagh were not as bad as they read in cold print. I was looked after by a nursing order of nuns, the Little Sisters of the Poor, and in particular by Sister Mary Finbar. She became my best friend, reading teacher, companion, nurse and spiritual mentor. She taught me how to pray, largely by her own holy example at the foot of my bed (17).

Looking back on the illness she nursed me through, I have often wondered what difference Sister Mary made. I think I know. If she had not prayed on my behalf in words similar to those in Psalm 6, *Be merciful to me Lord for I am faint; O Lord heal me for my bones are in agony*, I believe that I would not have made the full recovery which has allowed me to enjoy good health for the rest of my life. Like the psalmist, I know God listens to prayers for the sick.

A PRAYER BASED ON PSALM 6

Heavenly Father, have mercy upon me in my hour of illness. How long must I endure this physical, emotional, and spiritual pain? I am weak and exhausted. O Lord heal me, help me, save me.

But I know you will hear and accept my prayer. O Lord put my pains and my demons to flight. Give me that confidence which comes only from you. Through Jesus Christ our Lord. Amen.

PSALM 4: Pressure from friends falling out

For the director of music. With stringed instruments.
A psalm of David.

Answer me when I call to you,
   O my righteous God.
Give me relief from my distress;
   be merciful to me and hear my prayer.

[2] How long, O men, will you turn my glory into shame?
   How long will you love delusions and seek false gods?
Selah

[3] Know that the Lord has set apart the godly for himself;
   the Lord will hear when I call to him.

[4] In your anger do not sin;
   when you are on your beds,
   search your hearts and be silent.
Selah

[5] Offer right sacrifices
   and trust in the Lord.

[6] Many are asking, 'Who can show us any good?'
   Let the light of your face shine upon us, O Lord.
[7] You have filled my heart with greater joy
   than when their grain and new wine abound.
[8] I will lie down and sleep in peace,
   for you alone, O Lord,
   make me dwell in safety.

REFLECTION

This is a psalm which opens with a prayerful cry of distress to God and ends with warm expressions of praise and gratitude to him. In the middle verses the author has harsh words for worldly men who are turning his life into misery. We can use the analogy here of a sandwich with unpleasant man-made fillings enclosed between slices of good and Godly bread.

Let's start with a taster of those man-made fillings in the sandwich. The psalmist is upset by men who have humiliated him, lied about him and who hold wrong values. These are contemporary interpretations of the ancient poetic phrases about turning glory into shame, loving delusions and seeking false gods (verse 2). To make matters worse it appears that the men who are giving the psalmist all this grief were once his friends. Now they have become his angry and despondent adversaries (verses 4 and 6).

Because the Hebrew word for men in this context is often translated as 'wealthy men', it is a fair speculation that the author is writing about some merchants or business colleagues whose deals have gone sour. It is a familiar scenario. When those whose god is materialism encounter failure or unexpected falls in the market, they can become angry and despondent. Sometimes they lash out in their bitterness with lies and humiliating insults against former associates.

If this type of situation was the background to the pressure in the psalm, the author knew how to cope with it. For he was not a believer in the false god of materialism, but in the true God. That's why his top slice of bread in the sandwich was a humble prayer: *O my righteous God, give me relief from my distress, be merciful to me* (verse 1).

The final verses in the psalm suggest that the author's prayer was answered – not by a sudden improvement in his materialism but by his acceptance of a great spiritual truth. For he realises that God has filled his heart with far greater joy than anything which can be experienced by successful materialists. Compared to the pleasures of good harvests in ancient Israel, *when grain and new wine abound* (verse 7), or of good bonuses and profits in the 21st century market economy, the believer gains a far richer reward.

This reward is inner serenity, that peace which the world cannot give. To sleep in such peace secure in the knowledge that: *you alone O Lord make me dwell in safety* (verse 8), is part of the nourishment that comes from the Godly bread in this sandwich – the bread of life itself.

ADDITIONAL NOTES

Title and Form: *With stringed instruments. A psalm of David*: The musical references here indicate that this psalm was used for temple worship. This makes it less likely that it was personally written by King David. It is both a psalm of lament and a psalm of confidence.

Verses 2 and 4: *Selah*: This is a term which appears 71 times in the psalms at the end of certain verses. Its meaning is uncertain, but most scholars think it was a musical term indicating a change of tune or a raising of voices. It derives from the Hebrew root *sll*, meaning to lift up.

Verse 6: *Who can show us any good*: Probably refers to the agricultural good harvest of grain and new wine of verse 7.

Let the light of your face shine on us O Lord: Echoes the blessing of Aaron in Numbers 6: 22–26.

Verse 7: *when their grain and new wine abound*: Suggests that the men or wealthy men (see Reflection) referred to in verse 2 were farmers, vineyard owners, or agricultural merchants.

Verse 8: *You alone O lord make me dwell in safety*: When linked to Psalm 5: 8: *Lead me O Lord in your righteousness,* are the verses which inspired S. S. Wesley's much loved anthem 'Lead me Lord'.

PERSONAL COMMENT

For ten years I was Chairman of a merchant bank in the City of London and a director of several public companies in Britain and the USA. All of those companies had their ups and downs. Some of them occasionally ran into more serious troubles such as unexpected losses, hostile takeover bids and boardroom rows. So I am familiar with the commercial pressures that seem to form the background to this psalm.

Like the character in Henry Fielding's novel *Tom Jones*: 'who conversed so entirely about money that he thought it the only subject of importance in the world' (18), many business people are obsessed with the making of their fortunes. The Bible calls this the worship of Mammon.

There are two types of businessmen contrasted in this psalm. On the one hand we have the men or wealthy men of verse 2 who are Mammon-centred. They go to pieces when events, markets or harvests go wrong for them. Because money is their be-all and end-all they cannot cope with losing their wealth. When their *glory turns to shame* (verse 2), in terms of lost reputations or negative publicity, they are apt to become angry and blame others.

The psalmist was a target for his colleagues' blame and anger but he could handle these pressures because he was a different kind of businessman – God centred rather than Mammon-centred. I have known business people in both categories. The God-centred ones are much better at coping with the crises of their financial and personal lives. That is because they have a greater joy than amassing wealth in good times. While in bad times they sleep in peace, secure in the same knowledge and trust expressed in the psalmist's prayer: *for you alone O Lord make me dwell in safety* (verse 8).

A PRAYER BASED ON PSALM 4

O Lord hear my prayer and give me relief from my distress. I am being humiliated by those whose values are far removed from yours. They are angry and down because life is going wrong for them. Help me to stay peaceful because of my faith in you. Give me your joy which is greater than any worldly reward. The joy that comes from sleeping and waking with an inner peace, which only you can give. Through Jesus Christ Our Lord. Amen.

PSALM 17: Pressure from unjust accusers

A prayer of David.

Hear, O Lord, my righteous plea;
　　listen to my cry.
Give ear to my prayer –
　　it does not rise from deceitful lips.
[2] May my vindication come from you;
　　may your eyes see what is right.

[3] Though you probe my heart and examine me at night,
　　though you test me, you will find nothing;
　　I have resolved that my mouth will not sin.
[4] As for the deeds of men –
　　by the word of your lips
I have kept myself
　　from the ways of the violent.
[5] My steps have held to your paths;
　　my feet have not slipped.

[6] I call on you, O God, for you will answer me;
　　give ear to me and hear my prayer.
[7] Show the wonder of your great love,
　　you who save by your right hand
　　those who take refuge in you from their foes.
[8] Keep me as the apple of your eye;
　　hide me in the shadow of your wings
[9] from the wicked who assail me,
　　from my mortal enemies who surround me.

[10] They close up their callous hearts,
　　and their mouths speak with arrogance.
[11] They have tracked me down, they now surround me,
　　with eyes alert, to throw me to the ground.
[12] They are like a lion hungry for prey,
　　like a great lion crouching in cover.

[13] Rise up, O Lord, confront them, bring them down;
   rescue me from the wicked by your sword.
[14] O Lord, by your hand save me from such men,
   from men of this world whose reward is in this life.

You still the hunger of those you cherish;
   their sons have plenty,
   and they store up wealth for their children.
[15] And I – in righteousness I shall see your face;
   when I awake, I shall be satisfied with seeing your likeness.

REFLECTION

One of the worst forms of pressure can come from an unjust accusation. Innocent people often go to pieces in these circumstances. The author of this psalm protests vigorously, prays urgently, lurches into priggish self-righteousness and demands vengeance. Yet in the end he calms down and trusts God.

This psalm is a prayer, as the title tells us. It is the passionate plea of an innocent person under extreme pressure. Some scholars think it is the prayer of a falsely accused man on the eve of his trial. But the staccato demands of the psalmist have a wider application than the courtroom. Also his exhortations to God are so peremptory and at times so hysterical that they indicate a greater and more immediate danger than a legal battle.

The urgency of the prayer runs throughout the psalm as God is addressed in panic: *Hear O Lord, ... Listen ... Give ear*, begins verse 1. The tempo accelerates with appeals to *Rise up ... save me ... bring them down ... rescue me from the wicked by your sword* (verses 13–14).

What has produced this atmosphere of emergency is that the psalmist wants vindication from God and protection from his false accusers. He insists he is an innocent and truthful man. Some of his protestations of innocence make him sound as though he is putting himself forward as a sinless individual – which nobody is. Claims like: *though you test me you will find nothing* (verse 3), and *my feet have not slipped,* expose the author to the charge of self-righteousness. It seems unattractive but may be excusable if his pressures were sending him over the top into emotional and exaggerated self-justification.

Having appealed for his integrity and truthfulness to speak for themselves (verses 1–5), the psalmist makes a more personal appeal to God. *Show me the wonder of your great love* (verse 6), he prays. *Keep me as the apple of your eye, hide me in the shadow of your wings* (verse 8). These are beautiful words, immortalised down the centuries in the liturgy of the Catholic and Anglican Compline service.

Beauty, however, is followed by aggression, first towards the psalmist from his enemies and then the other way around. In verses 9–10 we are shown what Kidner calls 'an ugly scene of encirclement' (19) as mortal enemies track down their prey and move in for the kill.

Cornered and angry the psalmist prays for the destruction of his enemies by the sword. If this was literally his desire it seems an unacceptably violent form of vengeance, at odds with God's command in Deuteronomy 32: 35: *It is mine to avenge. I will repay.* However, it is possible that the author meant his prayer to be metaphorical and was expressing it with poetic licence.

In the final verse the mood changes to poetic confidence, if not poetic prophecy. For the psalmist has developed a calming sense of God's presence and reassurance. He makes the marvellous prediction: *in righteousness I shall see your face* (Verse 15). So in the end he knows that his honour will be vindicated. As C. H. Spurgeon has written: 'The smell of the furnace is on this psalm but there is evidence in the last verse that he who wrote it came unharmed out of the flame' (20). So may it be for all unjustly accused people who turn to this psalm in prayer and faith.

ADDITIONAL NOTES

Title and form: *A prayer of David*: Only three psalms (17, 86, 142) have this title which in each case is believed to show personal Davidic authorship. It is a prayer for vindication and for protection.

Verse 3: *examine me at night*: May refer to hours spent in nocturnal prayer or may denote sleepless introspection.

Verse 8: *apple of your eye*: Means the pupil, the symbol of what is to be protected and guarded with greatest care.

Verse 15: *in righteousness*: In the right, i.e., vindicated.

I shall see your face: Craig Broyles asks: 'How does this square with other Biblical claims that "you cannot see my face for no-one may see me and live"?' (Exodus 33: 20) (21). This answer is surely that this is a metaphor for being in God's presence.

when I awake: May mean an awakening from the restless sleep of the night (verse 3).

PERSONAL COMMENT

I know what it is like to be encircled by aggressive accusers. Even though I did not share David's innocence of all their charges, I was innocent of enough of them to be able to relate to the mood of this psalm.

Anyone whose way of life is threatened by false accusations (in my case pimping, illegal arms dealing and ministerial corruption) will go through different stages of mental anguish. These may include indignation, and a desire for revenge. But unless a truthful relationship with God is central to the wronged party's character, such human over reactions to the falsehoods can get out of hand and become self-inflicted wounds.

What saved this psalmist was the strength of his faithful relationship with God. He may have tested God's patience with the bossy and bellicose tone of some of his cries for deliverance (verse 13–14). On the other hand he must have pleased God by his integrity (verses 1–3) and by the spiritual beauty of his confident prayers (verses 7–8 and 15).

So the message of the psalm to a falsely accused person is: Come before God with a clean heart and conscience; ask for his help in prayer; and trust him absolutely. Then in the words of Psalm 37 (see page 7): *He will make your righteousness shine like the dawn, the justice of your cause like the noonday sun* (Psalm 37: 6).

A PRAYER BASED ON PSALM 17

O Lord hear my prayer. I am falsely accused by wicked people. Test me Lord and you will find that I am innocent. You will know that I am telling the truth. So come to my aid with your steadfast love and protect me from my accusers. Keep me as the apple of your eye. Hide me in the shadow of your wings. Vindicate my innocence and welcome me as I come through this nightmare into your loving presence.

Through Jesus Christ Our Lord. Amen.

PSALM 50, Verses 7–15: Pressure from religion

A psalm of Asaph.

[7] 'Hear, O my people, and I will speak,
   O Israel, and I will testify against you:
   I am God, your God.
[8] I do not rebuke you for your sacrifices
   or your burnt offerings, which are ever before me.
[9] I have no need of a bull from your stall
   or of goats from your pens,
[10] for every animal of the forest is mine,
   and the cattle on a thousand hills.
[11] I know every bird in the mountains,
   and the creatures of the field are mine.
[12] If I were hungry I would not tell you,
   for the world is mine, and all that is in it.
[13] Do I eat the flesh of bulls
   or drink the blood of goats?
[14] Sacrifice thank offerings to God,
   fulfil your vows to the Most High,
[15] and call upon me in the day of trouble;
   I will deliver you, and you will honour me.'

REFLECTION

People who 'get religion' sometimes manage to put themselves under pressure by trying to do too much to please God. It is a common fault which reoccurs down the ages, as these verses show. The psalmist seeks to correct the fault, first with a caricature of the wrong relationship between religious people and God, then with a summary of the right relationship.

This part of Psalm 50 begins with a solemn utterance from God in the role of principal witness for the prosecution. *I will testify against you,* he declares (verse 7). Surprisingly, what follows from the witness stand is not tough testimony but gentle humour at the expense of the over-religious. *I do not rebuke you* (verse 8), says God, for your sacrifices but do you think I really need them?

The pious people for whom the psalmist was writing had not stopped to think. Incredible though it seems, many ancient Israelites had come to believe that God actually required their offerings of slaughtered animals. To correct this misapprehension, the voice of the Lord speaks, first with omniscience and then with amusement.

God knows and owns everything he created. From the cattle on a thousand hills to every bird in the mountains; *they are mine* (verses 10–11), he proclaims. Then changing his tone almost into caricature, He wonders if his worshippers think of him as a hungry God anxiously awaiting a second helping of bull's flesh and an extra glass of goat's blood.

Before we laugh too loudly at the absurdities of Israelite cultic rituals in the first millennia BC, we should ponder on some of our rituals of religion in the 21st century AD. Whether they are in the form of high masses or happy clappy choruses, God does not need them any more than he needed ancient Israel's bulls and goats. For God looks behind the forms of religion and sees into the hearts of the religious.

If he sees in our religious practices sincere devotion and Godly dependency, God will be pleased. If he sees superficial commitment and spiritual emptiness, he will be disappointed. For God wants a relationship in which we give him our all. In return for our trust and obedience he gives his love and protection. This is the message in the last two verses of this extract from the psalm: *Fulfil your vows to the Most High and call upon me in the day of trouble. I will deliver you and you will honour me* (verses 14–15).

It is a neat summary of a right relationship with God. Religious people who feel under pressure to count the number of their gen-uflections or their guitar choruses are getting it wrong. God does not seek forms of worship that are calculated. He longs for the hearts of His worshippers to be filled with unconditional love.

ADDITIONAL NOTES

Title and form: The psalm as a whole is in the form of a temple liturgy. This extract is a divine speech beginning with a summons to obedience and ending with a promise.

Of Asaph: See note to Psalm 73.

Verse 6: *Selah*: See note to Psalm 4.

Verse 8: *I do not rebuke you*: God is rebuking not the practice of sacrifice but the motives of the sacrificers.

Verse 14: *Fulfil your vows to the Most High*: These vows were The Shema: 'Hear O Israel, The Lord our God is one...' (Deuteronomy 6: 4 *et seq.*) and the Decalogue or Ten Commandments (Deuteronomy 5: 6 *et seq.*)

PERSONAL COMMENT

Like many new Christians who feel they have made a new commitment or undergone a conversion experience I went through a period of over-the-top religiosity. In the winter of 1997–1998 I became fervent in my attendances of church services, prayer groups, Bible study programmes, and so on. Although this period coincided with the time when my political and legal dramas were at their worst, I don't think this was 'foxhole religion'. It was more a case of wanting to achieve 'results' in my quest to know the Lord. I was under the erroneous impression that such results would be related to the work I put into religious practices. So I made the mistake of trying to do too much too soon.

The counsellor who calmed me down from my excessive religious zeal (if I had been an ancient Israelite I am sure I would have been up there with the best of the bull and goat sacrificers!) was Charles W. Colson. He wrote to me in October 1997 in these terms:

> 'Somehow we think of conversions as being instantaneous. The moment when God regenerates us is. There is certainty about the fact that we are now His. But the conversion, that is the transformation from the old man to the new man, sometimes takes us a long while. There are lots of struggles that we inevitably go through. That is particularly true for strong-willed, able individuals like you and me. We have been so accustomed to thinking that we can do it on our own that it is very hard to release everything and simply trust God. But that is precisely what we must do. And we only learn to do that as we stumble and often grope in the dark. Don't be impatient with yourself ...' (22)

Colson's advice: 'simply trust God', is close to the words of Psalm 50 verse 15: *Call upon me in the day of trouble. I will deliver you.* Following this advice in faith will be a release for anyone under pressure from the excesses of formal or informal religion.

A PRAYER BASED ON PSALM 50

Lord you are the God of all creation. All the birds and beasts of the forest are yours. You know them all just as you know the cattle on a thousand hills.

So as you taught the ancient people of Israel that their animal sacrifice rituals without the right spiritual motives were meaningless, teach us to go about our religious practices with hearts that are committed and pleasing to you. As we fulfil our vows to you O Lord Most High, deliver us from evil when we call to you in the day of trouble, O Lord our Rock and our Redeemer. Amen.

PSALM 3: Pressure from enemies

A psalm of David. When he fled from his son Absalom.

O Lord, how many are my foes!
    How many rise up against me!
[2] Many are saying of me,
    'God will not deliver him.'
Selah

[3] But you are a shield around me, O Lord;
    you bestow glory on me and lift up my head.
[4] To the Lord I cry aloud,
    and he answers me from his holy hill.
Selah

[5] I lie down and sleep;
    I wake again, because the Lord sustains me.
[6] I will not fear the tens of thousands
    drawn up against me on every side.

[7] Arise, O Lord!
    Deliver me, O my God!
Strike all my enemies on the jaw;
    break the teeth of the wicked.

[8] From the Lord comes deliverance.
    May your blessing be on your people.
Selah

REFLECTION

This is a psalm about pressure from enemies. Although we may never have to face in our contemporary lives the sort of militaristic scenario described in these verses, we might find ourselves having unpleasant pressure applied to us in situations of personal confrontation or aggravation. So it is instructive to learn how the author of this psalm, King David, saw off his enemies with God's help.

The historical background to this psalm was a rebellion in Israel around 700 BC which nearly cost David his throne. It was led by the king's treacherous but favourite son, the handsome Absalom. After many political plots and military dramas, the rebellion was crushed and Absalom slain. However, David then became so paralysed with grief that he went to pieces, creating great unease and unrest among his people until God guided the kingdom into calmer times.

Although our personal troubles are likely to be on a smaller scale than David's, we can learn much from his response to a crisis. The psalm opens with the King praying for relief from pressure. He explains the size and nature of his problem. How many are my foes, attackers, and losers of confidence in me! (Verses 1 and 2). It is natural to launch such distress signals to God in times of trouble but they should be fired in faith.

David steadfastly believed that God would rescue him even if many others did not (verse 2). The next four verses reflect a rising spirit of confidence in the Lord's power. A good sleep (verse 5) played its part in this confidence building exercise which was founded on personal faith.

Faith, as St Paul's letter to the Hebrews reminds us, consists of 'being sure of what we hope for and certain of what we do not see' (Hebrews 11: 1). All that could be seen at the time on the political and military battlefields around Jerusalem was that everything was going wrong for the King. Absalom's revolt had forced David to flee from the city. But to a faithful believer the Lord was still there on his *holy hill* (verse 4) of Zion and in control of the situation. So David *cries aloud* or prays to God and gets an answer (verse 4).

The answer was evidently a big morale booster. For David comes out of his corner swinging the knockout punches of a champion boxer. *Strike all my enemies on the jaw; break the teeth of the wicked!* he demands (verse 7). This metaphor of a request for dental damage may sound rather excessively punitive at first hearing but the final verse of the psalm reveals the humility behind it. David is asking for victory not for himself, but for *your people* – i.e., God's (verse 8). The King recognises that if his purpose is not God's purpose there will be no success in his struggle to regain the throne, and no point to it either. So David's motivation and plea for victory is not self-centred but God-centred. This is why his prayers were answered.

This vital ingredient of keeping our purposes in tune with God's purposes needs to be remembered by all pray ers of the psalms, especially those who pray when under pressure from personal enemies.

ADDITIONAL NOTES

Title and Form: This is the first psalm to bear the title *Of David* and there are good grounds for the view of many scholars that he wrote it himself. He is thought to have composed poems in the aftermath of military battles, among them his beautiful lament for Saul and Jonathan (2 Samuel 1: 19–27). The story on which this psalm is based, the rebellion of his son Absalom, is told in 2 Samuel 15–19. It is a protective psalm, a plea for deliverance from danger.

Verse 4: holy hill: This is a reference to Mount Zion, God's holy dwelling place in Jerusalem. It was a heavenly rather than an earthly locality, although in physical terms the ark of the covenant symbolised the divine presence.

Verses 2, 4, 8: Selah: See note to Psalm 4.

PERSONAL COMMENT

A new phrase I picked up in prison was 'under the cosh'. It means being under pressure, feeling the heat, or going through a period of great stress. Inevitably there are wielders of the cosh too, and they are easy to personalise and demonise as enemies.

Everyone, from Kings to convicts, can find themselves suffering at the hands of enemies. The New Testament tells us to 'turn the other cheek' (Matthew 5: 39) when they give us aggravation. This is not always easy to do. Our human nature impels us to hit back, but we should not get into the business of revenge. As the God of ancient Israel reminded his people, that is his business: 'It is mine to avenge, I will repay' (Deuteronomy 32: 35).

In this psalm David sounds close to wanting vengeance when he asks for his enemies to be struck on the jaw. But the saving grace here is that *the wicked* (verse 7) were God's enemies too.

David never forgot that he was God's man, working with the grain of God's purposes. When I used to get into fights against enemies I was doing so for my own purposes. That was wrong. David's appeals to God were right.

A PRAYER BASED ON PSALM 3

O Lord I seem to be surrounded by hostile foes. Put your shield of protection around me when I sleep and when I wake so that I have no fear. Give me answers to my problems from your heavenly throne. Deliver me from evil in accordance with your will and purpose. Through Jesus Christ Our Lord. Amen.

PSALM 123: Pressure from ridicule and contempt

A song of ascents.

I lift up my eyes to you,
   to you whose throne is in heaven.
[2] As the eyes of slaves look to the hand of their master,
   as the eyes of a maid look to the hand of her mistress,
so our eyes look to the Lord our God,
   till he shows us his mercy.

[3] Have mercy on us, O Lord, have mercy on us,
   for we have endured much contempt.
[4] We have endured much ridicule from the proud,
   much contempt from the arrogant.

REFLECTION

Ridicule and contempt are hard to deal with whether for an individual, for a group, or for a nation. In the sermon on the mount the epithet *You fool!* was singled out as the most hurtful of insults (Matthew 5: 22). In our contemporary society it can be easier to cope emotionally with head-on criticism than it is to suffer contempt from lofty lips or scorn from the e-mails and editorials of the arrogant. The psalmist had an instinctive understanding of such emotions, and of how to pray about them.

The psalm opens in a form similar to the Lord's prayer. The eyes of the supplicant are lifted far above the hills of Psalm 121 to the heavenly throne (verse 2). Then comes a rather stilted comparison with the eyes of a slave on his master which Derek Kidner felicitously refines to: 'the trained watchfulness of the servant who is ready for the smallest gesture' (23).

At the heart of the psalm is a poignant plea enhanced by the double repetition which is such a significant form of emphasis in Hebrew:

Have mercy on us O Lord have mercy on us
For we have endured much contempt
We have endured much ridicule (verses 3–4).

What makes these blows worse is that they are coming not from an equal but from the proud and arrogant (verse 4). The author and the people of Israel, on whose behalf he is writing, feel hurt.

Historically it is thought that this psalm derives from the episode, recounted by Nehemiah, of Sanballat and his associates who 'mocked and ridiculed' the efforts of the inhabitants of Jerusalem to rebuild the city wall after the exile (Nehemiah 2: 19; 4: 1). However, the prayer is just as valid for any situation in which arrogant voices pour scorn on a righteous cause or man. In the modern world the vilification of a decent individual or group of people happens all too often.

Arrogant voices cannot easily be answered back. So those who suffer under the lash of their ridicule and contempt have only one spiritual option. They should pray, as the psalmist did, for mercy from the God who vindicates a right cause, abhors wrongdoing and despises the proud.

ADDITIONAL NOTES

Form and Title: This is the fourth of fifteen psalms (120–134) which have the title *A song of ascents*. For further comment on the title see note on Psalm 130. This is a lament psalm expressed in the form of a prayer for deliverance.

Verse 1: *to you whose throne is in heaven*: This is an unusual form of address although it is echoed in Isaiah's vision of the Lord 'seated on a throne high and exalted' (Isaiah 6: 1).

Verse 2: Scholars are divided over whether the hand of the master and mistress is a reference to the proud and arrogant rulers, or to the hand of the Lord which should be watched so that every gesture may be obeyed. Kidner's interpretation (see Reflection) seems the best bet.

Verses 3–4: The distress is ridicule and contempt. The sole petition is for mercy. The prayer could refer to some unknown humiliation during the exile or to the Sanballat episode described in Nehemiah 2–4 (see Reflection). In any event, the prayer is not so much individual as national for the use of the words *we* and *our* suggest that the psalmist is speaking for the people of Israel.

PERSONAL COMMENT

The Common Law definition of a libel is that it is a statement which brings someone into 'hatred, ridicule and contempt'. I felt libelled when I was falsely accused of being a pimp, an arms dealer and a corrupt Minister. But I wish I had lifted my eyes up to the Lord rather than to the Law Courts as he might have reminded me of my own shortcomings and weaknesses.

Having been the object of a great deal of ridicule and contempt in recent years, some of it deserved, I know it hurts. So I can empathise with the psalmist. He prays not for revenge nor for any specific remedy. His is the humblest and simplest of prayers; *Have mercy on us O Lord*. It is a request which a merciful God loves to grant.

A PRAYER BASED ON PSALM 123

O Lord we are being subjected to ridicule and contempt by proud and arrogant people. So we lift up our eyes to your heavenly throne and humbly ask: Lord have mercy on us, Lord have mercy on us. Amen.

PSALM 84: Pressures of love and separation

For the director of music. According to gittith.
Of the Sons of Korah. A psalm.

How lovely is your dwelling-place,
  O Lord Almighty!
[2] My soul yearns, even faints,
  for the courts of the Lord;
my heart and my flesh cry out
  for the living God.

[3] Even the sparrow has found a home,
  and the swallow a nest for herself,
  where she may have her young –
a place near your altar,
  O Lord Almighty, my King and my God.
[4] Blessed are those who dwell in your house;
  they are ever praising you.
Selah

[5] Blessed are those whose strength is in you,
  who have set their hearts on pilgrimage.
[6] As they pass through the Valley of Baca,
  they make it a place of springs,
  the autumn rains also cover it with pools.
[7] They go from strength to strength,
  till each appears before God in Zion.

[8] Hear my prayer, O Lord God Almighty;
  listen to me, O God of Jacob.
Selah

[9] Look upon our shield, O God;
  look with favour on your anointed one.

[10] Better is one day in your courts
  than a thousand elsewhere;
I would rather be a doorkeeper in the house of my God
  than dwell in the tents of the wicked.

[11] For the Lord God is a sun and shield;
    the Lord bestows favour and honour;
no good thing does he withhold
    from those whose walk is blameless.
[12] O Lord Almighty,
    blessed is the man who trusts in you.

REFLECTION

Love can create its own pressures, especially when the beloved is far away. This psalm is all about the longings and yearnings of love. However the object of the author's strong emotions was not a person, but a house – the house of God.

The psalm opens in the poignant poetry of separated love. The author's heart, soul and flesh are aching to be in the dwelling place of the Lord – the temple – but for some unexplained reason this desire is unfulfilled. So the psalmist yearns to change places with one of the swallows or sparrows (verse 3) who flew in and out of the temple's open airy courtyards and nested in its eaves.

Beautiful though these verses are, it is difficult for a modern mind to comprehend the homesickness that afflicted this author. But as we saw in Psalm 42 and 43 (which may have been written by the same hand) a servant of the temple could suffer the most painful withdrawal symptoms if prevented from going back to his religious duties there.

The changing mood of the psalm can be tracked through its beatitudes in which the word *Blessed* is used three times, once with longing (verse 4); once with strength (verse 5); and once with trust (verse 12).

The longing moves from birds to people as the psalmist thinks wistfully of those who live in God's house, *ever singing your praise* (verse 4).

Then in a change of mood the author pulls himself out of his lovesick reveries and becomes resolute. He thinks of the pilgrims who gain the strength they need for their arduous journeys from their love of God (verse 5).

Although the reference in the next verse to the *Valley of Baca* (a vale of lamentation – see notes, below) and its springs is obscure in the NIV version of the Bible, it comes alive with meaning in Miles Coverdale's matchless translation in the *Book of Common Prayer*: 'Who going through the vale of misery use it for a well'. The idea behind either translation is this: Blessed is the individual who can use his or her tears of misery as a well or spring from which to drink the waters of spiritual refreshment. Anyone under pressure from sadness should take strength, as the psalmist did, from pondering on this idea. For adversity is often the gateway to a deeper faith.

Fortified by the wellsprings of his misery the author starts to pray for himself (verse 8) and for the King, *the anointed one* (verse 9 – see note following). He tells God that he would rather be a mere temple doorkeeper for only one day than to spend a thousand days in comfort elsewhere with ungodly or wicked people.

The psalm concludes with a rich verse of praise for God (verse 11) and a final statement of who is *Blessed* (verse 12). The author sees that this state of blessedness is not just for temple priests or pilgrims, but for everyone who trusts in God.

ADDITIONAL NOTES

Form and Title: This is both a temple psalm and a pilgrimage psalm.

According to gittith: Gittith is the feminine of gath, a word meaning wine-press. Scholars have speculated that in this context gittith is a tune or instrument or ceremony connected with the wine harvest which coincided with the temple Feast of the Tabernacles. Alternatively it could be a tune taking its name from Gath, a Philistine town.

Of the Korahites: See note to Psalm 42 on page 25.

Verse 3: *sparrow, swallow*: Small birds who nested in the eaves of the temple and flew round its altars. The psalmist is not depicting a derelict building. Many courtyards of the temple were open air structures.

Verse 5: *highways to Zion*: Could refer either to pilgrims knowing the roads to Jerusalem, or to believers knowing God in their hearts.

Verse 6: *Valley of Baca*: The name may derive from the Hebrew verb bākāh, meaning to weep. Alternatively, because the noun is the singular of the word meaning balsam trees, it may refer to the only known vale of such trees, the vale of Rephaim where a dejected David was wonderfully refreshed (2 Samuel 5: 23). So vale of misery or vale of refreshing springs, best translated by Coverdale (see Reflection).

pools: 'blessings' is an alternative translation.

Verses 4 and 8: *Selah*: A musical term meaning change of voices.

Verse 9: *the face of your anointed*: A reference to the King, but why does it appear in this highly personal psalm? Kidner thinks it has 'the look of a parenthesis' (24), possibly referring to some national tragedy involving the King. Stott suggests that the nation's welfare may have been bound up in the King's (25).

Verse 10: *Doorkeeper*: May have been the psalmist's past occupation.

Wicked: Those who do not honour God.

Verse 12: This final verse, whose Beatitude encompasses all those who have never entered the temple as priests or pilgrims, brings to mind Jesus' words to Thomas: 'Blessed are those who have not seen and yet have believed' (John 20: 29).

PERSONAL COMMENT

Verse 6 of this psalm struck a deep chord with me once I had deciphered the Baca reference and accepted the Coverdale translation: 'Who going through the vale of misery use it for a well'.

We all go through vales of misery in life. Can we use them to turn our tears into a well from which to draw the water of life? It is a thought that strengthened the psalmist and many other sorrowing believers. As Luther put it: 'It is in our pain and in our brokenness that we come closest to Christ' (26).

When my sorrows (defeat, disgrace, divorce, bankruptcy and jail) were coming at me, 'not as single spies but in battalions' (27) to use Shakespeare's words, I shed many tears. But I also started searching for spiritual strength and refreshment. Some of those searchings were in retrospect excessive, others led me to the gold seam of a committed faith. In the middle of these slightly frenzied activities I was asked to write a major annual article for the

Spectator known as 'The Christmas Meditation'. This was its penultimate paragraph:

'On the subject of caricatures I must admit to a worry in recent weeks that I might have been developing one or two caricaturable religious tendencies myself. Belonging as I do to the Church Reticent wing of Anglicanism, I am suspicious of foxhole conversions through easy believism and cautious about accepting adversity as the gateway to a deeper faith. So time and time again in all sorts of very different Christian settings I have inwardly asked the sceptical question "What on earth am I doing here?" The answer, in so far as I can search for one, may be found in a verse from The Psalms which says that if you are going through a vale of misery, then use it for a well ...'(28).

Digging the well and filling it with tears can be a slow and agonising process. Yet as both I and the psalmist discovered, the view of your life looks different when you have accepted God's spiritual refreshment and put your trust in Him.

A PRAYER BASED ON PSALM 84

O Lord I am unhappy because of strange longings and yearnings. I envy those who dwell in you.

As I search for you, teach me to understand that while I go through a vale of misery I may be able to use it as a well of spiritual refreshment.

So hear my prayer Lord. I would rather have a life of service with you than be a worldly success without you. Help me to walk with you, trust in you, and dwell in you. For in these ways I know I will find the true wellsprings of peace and contentment. Through Jesus Christ Our Lord. Amen.

PSALM 32: Pressure relieved by God's forgiveness

Of David. A maskil.

Blessed is he
>whose transgressions are forgiven,
>whose sins are covered.

[2] Blessed is the man
>whose sin the Lord does not count against him
>and in whose spirit is no deceit.

[3] When I kept silent,
>my bones wasted away
>through my groaning all day long.

[4] For day and night
>your hand was heavy upon me;

my strength was sapped
>as in the heat of summer.

Selah

[5] Then I acknowledged my sin to you
>and did not cover up my iniquity.

I said, 'I will confess
>my transgressions to the Lord' –

and you forgave
>the guilt of my sin.

Selah

[6] Therefore let everyone who is godly pray to you
>while you may be found;

surely when the mighty waters rise,
>they will not reach him.

[7] You are my hiding-place;
>you will protect me from trouble
>and surround me with songs of deliverance.

Selah

[8] I will instruct you and teach you in the way you should go;
>I will counsel you and watch over you.

[9] Do not be like the horse or the mule,
    which have no understanding
but must be controlled by bit and bridle
    or they will not come to you.
[10] Many are the woes of the wicked,
    but the Lord's unfailing love
    surrounds the man who trusts in him.
[11] Rejoice in the Lord and be glad, you righteous;
    sing, all you who are upright in heart!

REFLECTION

This psalm was written by a man who was rejoicing with happiness because he had been liberated from a pressure so acute that it was making him ill. What was the pressure? What was the secret of his freedom and his happiness?

After a couple of opening beatitudes (of which more later) the real story behind the psalm is told in verses 3–5. The author was laid low with a debilitating illness. He was groaning, his bones were aching and his strength was sapped. The cause of his problem was that he had *kept silent* (verse 3) about some unknown but great sin. So he was suffering from psychosomatic symptoms brought on by suppressed guilt.

Having given the diagnosis the author switches to a personal testimony of repentance. He confessed his sin fully and penitently to the Lord. The speed of the Lord's forgiveness was stunning. St Augustine of Hippo, who loved this psalm, wrote of verse 5: 'The word is scarcely in his mouth before the wound is healed' (29). No wonder the psalmist began rejoicing and singing!

The forgiven sinner's joy took several forms. It resulted in the writing of this psalm which opens with the resounding declarations of spiritual truth. In shorthand form the beatitudes in verses 1 and 2 say: Happy (or blessed) is the man whose sins no longer count against him in the eyes of God because he has received forgiveness.

The psalmist cannot wait to share his good news with anyone willing to listen to him. He advises other people under pressure to start praying (verse 6) to the God who has been his protector. Then the voice of God enters the psalm to say: *I will instruct you, teach you, counsel you and watch over you* (verse 8). The four verbs create a picture of a loving father bringing up a young son, never taking his eye off the boy.

The message of the psalm is that God the Father embraces his penitent children with loving intimacy. In return those children adore their heavenly father because he has freed them from their guilt and given them a new start in life. So it is a happy psalm beginning and ending in joy. In the middle the author tells the personal story of his God-centred journey to forgiveness which many a sinner under pressure should emulate.

ADDITIONAL NOTES

Form and title: Although Christian tradition classified this as one of the penitential psalms (the others are 6, 32, 38, 51, 102, 130, 143), it is more a psalm of personal thanksgiving for God's forgiveness.

A Maskil: A musical term, but some scholars think the description also indicated fine writing because the word can be translated 'a psalm of understanding'. This would fit well here.

Of David: There is speculation that this psalm is a refined and later version of the King's penitence over the Bathsheba saga (see Reflection to Psalm 51 on pages 30–32).

Verses 1 and 2: *Covered* means blotted out, expunged from the record. For biblical meanings of sin transgression and iniquity (verse 5) see Psalm 51 on pages 28–29.

Verse 6: *while you may be found*: Is better translated in other versions of the Bible as 'at a time of stress' or 'in the hour of anxiety'. These phrases give a clearer indication of how an individual feels when the waters of trouble are rising around him.

Verse 9: *horse or mule*: This verse may be a refinement of the wisdom teaching in Proverbs 26: 3 – *a whip for the horse, a bridle for an ass, the rod for a fool's back*.

The Psalm as a whole: St Paul quotes the opening verses of this psalm in Romans 4: 6–8 as an Old Testament example of his New Testament proclamation that God justifies the sinner by the gift of his grace through faith apart from works.

PERSONAL COMMENT

Like the psalmist I have known the pain of guilt, the relief of penitence and the happiness of forgiveness. One of the greatest blessings this confers is a feeling of intimacy with God, captured in verses 7–8.

One other writer who highlights the intimacy of penitence is William Temple (1881–1945) who many regard as the greatest Archbishop of Canterbury of the 20th century. He wrote in his *Palm Sunday to Easter*: 'It is penitence which creates intimacy with our Lord. No one can know him intimately who has not realised the sickness of his own soul and obtained healing from the physician of souls. Our virtues do not bring us near to Christ – the gulf between them and his holiness remain unbridgeable. Our science does not bring us near him nor our art. Our pain may give us a taste of fellowship with Him but it is only a taste unless that great creator of intimacy – penitence – is also there' (30).

Another link between this psalm and my own experiences is the joy of penitence. I have written about this phenomenon in my personal comment on Psalm 51. I find these similarities across the millennia amazing. A few years ago if anyone had asked me what I would do, in the unlikely event of confessing my sins, immediately afterwards I would have said 'keep quiet about it'. The idea of public rejoicing after penitence (verse 11) or advising others to make the same journey of prayer (verse 6) would have seemed out of the question. Something has changed me. Perhaps it is the same God-given power that changed the psalmist.

A PRAYER BASED ON PSALM 32

Heavenly Father, thank you for your willingness to forgive us our sins, and to grant us the life-changing happiness that comes from intimacy with you.

Thank you for your teachings, your guidance, and your watchfulness over our lives. We rejoice and sing your praises, O God of forgiveness, mercy and grace.

Through Our Lord and Saviour Jesus Christ. Amen.

PSALM 27: How to stay confident under attack

Of David.

The Lord is my light and my salvation –
    whom shall I fear?
The Lord is the stronghold of my life –
    of whom shall I be afraid?
[2] When evil men advance against me
    to devour my flesh,
when my enemies and my foes attack me,
    they will stumble and fall.
[3] Though an army besiege me,
    my heart will not fear;
though war break out against me,
    even then will I be confident.

[4] One thing I ask of the Lord,
    this is what I seek:
that I may dwell in the house of the Lord
    all the days of my life,
to gaze upon the beauty of the Lord
    and to seek him in his temple.
[5] For in the day of trouble
    he will keep me safe in his dwelling;
he will hide me in the shelter of his tabernacle
    and set me high upon a rock.
[6] Then my head will be exalted
    above the enemies who surround me;
at his tabernacle will I sacrifice with shouts of joy;
    I will sing and make music to the Lord.

[7] Hear my voice when I call, O Lord;
    be merciful to me and answer me.
[8] My heart says of you, 'Seek his face!'
    Your face, Lord, I will seek.
[9] Do not hide your face from me,

do not turn your servant away in anger;
  you have been my helper.
Do not reject me or forsake me,
  O God my Saviour.
[10] Though my father and mother forsake me,
  the Lord will receive me.
[11] Teach me your way, O Lord;
  lead me in a straight path
  because of my oppressors.
[12] Do not hand me over to the desire of my foes,
  for false witnesses rise up against me,
  breathing out violence.
[13] I am still confident of this:
  I will see the goodness of the Lord
  in the land of the living.
[14] Wait for the Lord;
  be strong and take heart
  and wait for the Lord.

REFLECTION

This is a psalm about finding the confidence to rise above enemies. This is not as easy as the author makes it sound in the opening verses. For confidence is rarely a seamless garment. It can fade or have holes torn in it when the pressure is on. Later parts of the psalm concede this. But the author seeks and finds the path to ultimate confidence.

The psalm opens on a note of sublime trust. Using the device of the rhetorical question the author declares that since God is his light, his salvation and his stronghold: *of whom then shall I be afraid?* (verses 1–2).

Yet there are quite a few things happening in his life which might make anyone feel scared. He is under attack from evil men, enemies, foes, a besieging army, oppressors, false witnesses, and perpetrators of violence (verses 2, 3, 11, 12). Some of these attackers are no doubt portrayed poetically rather than literally, but the general picture is clear. The psalmist is under heavy pressure.

In the first part of the psalm the author's confidence in the face of his pressures remains unshaken: *My head will be exalted above the enemies who surround me* (verse 6) he sings. But then his tone changes. The next six verses are a prayer of anguish. His confidence may not be destroyed but it is evidently ebbing away. For the psalmist cries out for mercy, begging God not to turn away from him, reject him, forsake him, or hand him over to his foes (verses 7–12).

These dark moments of despair are terrifying given the formidable line-up of enemies the psalmist is facing. But in the final verses his inner courage reasserts itself, so much so that he announces: *I am still confident ... be strong and take heart* (verse 14). So that regained confidence enabled him to see off all those evil forces. How did he do it?

The answer lies in a key word which appears four times in this psalm – seeking. The author's strength comes from being a seeker. He is single minded. *One thing* is what he is after, although he expresses it in four different ways. First he is seeking a constant relationship with God. This is his wish to *dwell in the house of the Lord all the days of my life* (verse 4). This does not literally mean taking up occupation as a live-in servant of the church or temple. It means the fulfilment of the last line of Archbishop Cranmer's Communion Service prayer of humble access: 'that we may evermore dwell in him and he in us'. That is as good a definition as any of a constant relationship with God.

As a result of his relationship with God the author wants to seek him in his temple and to gaze upon the beauty of his holiness (verse 4). Today this might mean seeking God through worship, through contemplative prayer, or through adoration and thanksgiving for the beauty of his creation. There are many paths open to seekers. But in time of trouble we seek God's face. The relationship becomes urgent and personal. God doesn't always reveal himself immediately, and he did not do so to the psalmist who cried out: *Do not hide your face from me. Do not turn away from your servant in anger* (verse 9) – perhaps a hint that the servant knew he had sinned. But at the end of the day God delivered. Confidence in *the goodness of the Lord* returned. So may it be for all who truly seek to *dwell in the house of the Lord*.

ADDITIONAL NOTES

Form and title: Some scholars, pre eminently Herman Gunkel, assert that Psalm 27 was originally two psalms, verses 1–6 being a psalm of confidence and verses 7–14 being an individual lament psalm. But there are strong arguments for believing that the two parts were deliberately bound together for both spiritual and liturgical reasons.

Of David: This psalm could refer to episodes in the King's life such as his pursuit by Saul or his flight from Absalom, so there is a case for personal Davidic authorship.

Verse 1: *light, salvation, stronghold* are three words that dispel anxiety and instil confidence. They are frequently used in the psalms.

Verse 2–3: The various enemies and evildoers are portrayed here metaphorically as terrifying animalistic figures, not as humans. They will stumble and fall because God is protecting the psalmist.

Verse 4: *that I may dwell in the house of the Lord all the days of my life* should be taken figuratively and not as the psalmist's literal ambition (*cf.* Psalm 23, verse 6, and Reflection).

Verse 5 & 6: *tabernacle*: The holiest of holy places in the temple where no enemy would dare to go, and where the most important sacrifices were made.

Verse 10: *though my mother and father forsake me*: This is a hypothetical suggestion says Kidner: 'not that both of David's parents have in fact disowned him but that beyond their breaking point the love of God will still persist' (31).

Verse 14: *Be strong*, etc: An echo of the Lord's command to Joshua: 'Be strong and of good courage' (Joshua 1: 6 and 9).

PERSONAL COMMENT

I used to have plenty of enemies, particularly in the media. At the time of my political dramas I imagined they were eager to *devour my flesh* (verse 2). But in reality they were not that bad even though I now wish I had been blessed with the spiritual confidence to rise above them.

These days in my work as a trustee of the charity Christian Solidarity Worldwide I travel the world to support men and women of faith who are being persecuted by real enemies. This psalm has historically given comfort and confidence to Christians suffering persecution. On October 28th 1885, the day before Bishop James Harrington met a martyr's death in Equatorial Africa, he wrote in his journal: 'I am quite broken down and brought low. Comforted by Psalm 27.'

That supreme spiritual comfort in the face of terrible physical persecution comes from a constant relationship with the Lord. I have met persecuted Christians from countries like North Korea, Indonesia, Laos and China who are suffering for their faith in the 21st century. One thing they seem to have in common is a holy confidence that their relationship with God will protect them and lift them above their enemies.

Many confident believers start their journeys as stumbling seekers. When I was starting to search for God I remember how two verses from Jeremiah leapt out at me from the pages of my Bible: 'Then you will call upon me and come to pray to me and I will listen to you. You will seek me and find me when you seek me with all your heart' (Jeremiah 29: 12–13).

In my experience, when the seeking turns into a wholehearted commitment you know you have been granted God's grace and entered into a real relationship with him. From that knowledge comes the confidence, so beautifully expressed in the opening verses of this psalm, that no enemy should be feared.

A PRAYER BASED ON PSALM 27

O Lord you are my light and my salvation. Why should I fear my enemies? With you as my rock, why should I ever feel afraid?

But in my times of human weakness and trouble, Lord be merciful to me and answer my prayers. For I seek you with all my heart. I seek a constant relationship with you.

So teach me your way O Lord. Grant me a strong heart to rise above my enemies as I wait for you, my Lord and Saviour, with confidence. Amen.

PSALM 40, Verses 1–11: A tonic for people under pressure

For the director of music. Of David. A psalm.

I waited patiently for the Lord;
    he turned to me and heard my cry.
[2] He lifted me out of the slimy pit,
    out of the mud and mire;
he set my feet on a rock
    and gave me a firm place to stand.
[3] He put a new song in my mouth,
    a hymn of praise to our God.
Many will see and fear
    and put their trust in the Lord.

[4] Blessed is the man
    who makes the Lord his trust,
who does not look to the proud,
    to those who turn aside to false gods.
[5] Many, O Lord my God,
    are the wonders you have done.
The things you planned for us
    no-one can recount to you;
were I to speak and tell of them,
    they would be too many to declare.
[6] Sacrifice and offering you did not desire,
    but my ears you have pierced;
burnt offerings and sin offerings
    you did not require.
[7] Then I said, 'Here I am, I have come –
    it is written about me in the scroll.
[8] I desire to do your will, O my God;
    your law is within my heart.'

[9] I proclaim righteousness in the great assembly;
    I do not seal my lips,
    as you know, O Lord.

[10] I do not hide your righteousness in my heart;
   I speak of your faithfulness and salvation.
I do not conceal your love and your truth
   from the great assembly.

[11] Do not withhold your mercy from me, O Lord;
   may your love and your truth always protect me.

REFLECTION

This psalm should be a tonic for people under pressure. In the form of a personal testimony it tells how God rescues those who cry out to Him in desperate circumstances. The giver of the testimony also expands on the subsequent joy he has found in his life as a result of obeying God and of giving public witness about divine salvation. It makes a powerful piece of spiritual autobiography.

The psalm opens with a picture of a man stuck in a slimy pit of mud and mire (verse 2). The language evokes a stinking cesspool but it can cover any sort of personal mess or disaster which we might fall into at some stage of our lives.

Although he is sinking into this morass, the autobiographer manages to wait for the Lord, not in panic but *patiently* (verse 1). His trust is justified. God hears his prayer, pulls him out of the slime, sets his feet on a rock and puts a new song in his mouth which causes many others to believe.

Audiences appreciate authentic testimonies. This one is rooted in real experience leading to real change. The key to the psalm is verses 6–8 which start with a rather baffling reference to having ears pierced. This has nothing to do with modern jewellery fashions! It means that the author's ears were opened to God's word as a result of being rescued from the pit.

The first message those newly opened ears heard, is that the ancient rituals of animal sacrifices were unimportant to God. What God wants is obedience to his will – from the heart (verse 8). The sudden desire to do God's will was the tipping point of the psalmist's journey. So it should be in ours.

Having made a commitment of obedience to God, the psalmist becomes a public proclaimer of his message. Instead of floundering on his own in the mud and mire he stands up in the great assembly (a metaphor meaning 'before the world') and gives his testimony. He bears witness, from his personal experiences to the power of God's love, truth, faithfulness and salvation (verses 10–11).

Although this particular story may have made great impact in ancient Israel because it is thought to have come from the lips of King David, many comparable testimonies are given in the 21st century on the airwaves, in books and magazines, and in church talks. He that has ears to hear, let him hear.

ADDITIONAL NOTES

Title and Form: *Of David*: The superscription in this psalm is thought by many scholars to denote the King's personal authorship. See note to *In the scroll* (verse 7) below.

Verse 2: *The slimy pit*: With its mud and mire have strong echoes of Jeremiah's experiences in the cistern (Jeremiah 38: 6). But the imagery could refer to any sort of disaster scenario from personal depression to military catastrophe.

Verse 6: *My ears you have pierced*: Is thought to have parallels with the expressions used in Isaiah 50: 4 *et seq.*: 'he wakens my ear', 'the Lord God has opened my ear'.

Verse 7: *In the scroll*: These words are thought to be a reference to the Deuteronomic law of Kings, (see Deuteronomy 17: 14–20) which imposed certain cultic requirements on the Kings of Israel including writing *on a scroll* (Deuteronomy 17: 18). This allusion is the principal reason why this psalm is believed to be a royal liturgy of thanksgiving for deliverance, personally composed by David.

Another pointer to the royal antecedents of this psalm is that verses 6–8 are thought to be a reminder of the events described in 1 Samuel 15. Saul, Israel's first King, forfeited the throne because he went through the motions of offering sacrifice while acting disobediently. *To obey is better than to sacrifice* (1 Samuel 15: 22) was a warning from Elijah, certain to have been heeded by Saul's successor, David.

Verses 6–8: This passage of the psalm is quoted in Hebrews 10: 5–7. The author of Hebrews puts the quotation into the mouth of Christ with the explanation that animal sacrifice was to be replaced by Christ-like obedience.

Verse 9: *the great assembly*: May mean the great congregation of God's faithful people in the temple, or 'the nation' or simply 'in public'.

Rest of the psalm: There is a second half of this psalm (verses 11–17) which is a prayer for deliverance. It also appears again in the Psalter as Psalm 70. Very different in tone to verses 1–11, it appears to be a separate and later addition.

PERSONAL COMMENT

I can identify both with the psalmist's *slimy pit* (a perfectly good metaphor for a prison cell) and with his desire to give public witness about God's loving kindness after being rescued.

When I came out of prison I was advised by one newspaper columnist 'to shut up and follow Jack Profumo's example' (32). This meant a life of self-effacing charity work – the much admired course of action followed for the last forty years by John Profumo the ex-Minister who fell into political disgrace in the 1960s after telling a lie in a personal statement to the House of Commons.

In some ways such a route to redemption would have been far easier than the one I chose. Studying theology and then going into Christian lay ministry (mainly in prisons and for the persecuted Church) had its difficulties, particularly when I started to be in demand as a testimony speaker. However, I came round to the psalmist's views about 'proclaiming' or giving public witness so now I do a fair amount of Christian outreach speaking. Why? Because I agree with these words from John Stott about Psalm 40: 'When God sets our feet on the rock and puts his law in our ear and in our hearts, we cannot keep our lips from making His goodness known' (33).

A PRAYER BASED ON PSALM 40

Lord you lifted me out of the pit of my despair. You rescued me, changed me, and set my feet upon the rock of your truth. All I now want to do is to keep your laws and to obey your will. If it is your will, help me to tell the world about the saving power of your love. Through Jesus Christ Our Lord. Amen.

PART III

UNDERSTANDING GOD
WHEN UNDER PRESSURE

PSALM 19: God reveals himself

For the director of music. A psalm of David.

The heavens declare the glory of God;
  the skies proclaim the work of his hands.
[2] Day after day they pour forth speech;
  night after night they display knowledge.
[3] There is no speech or language
  where their voice is not heard.
[4] Their voice goes out into all the earth,
  their words to the ends of the world.

In the heavens he has pitched a tent for the sun,
  [5] which is like a bridegroom coming forth from his pavilion,
  like a champion rejoicing to run his course.
[6] It rises at one end of the heavens
  and makes its circuit to the other;
  nothing is hidden from its heat.

[7] The law of the Lord is perfect,
  reviving the soul.
The statutes of the Lord are trustworthy,
  making wise the simple.
[8] The precepts of the Lord are right,
  giving joy to the heart.
The commands of the Lord are radiant,
  giving light to the eyes.
[9] The fear of the Lord is pure,
  enduring for ever.
The ordinances of the Lord are sure
  and altogether righteous.
[10] They are more precious than gold,
  than much pure gold;
they are sweeter than honey,
  than honey from the comb.
[11] By them is your servant warned;
  in keeping them there is great reward.

[12] Who can discern his errors?
   Forgive my hidden faults.
[13] Keep your servant also from wilful sins;
   may they not rule over me.
Then will I be blameless,
   innocent of great transgression.

[14] May the words of my mouth and the meditation of my
         heart
   be pleasing in your sight,
   O Lord, my Rock and my Redeemer.

REFLECTION

The best way of trying to understand God is to observe and learn from what he has revealed to us. This psalm gives the most powerful portrayal of the doctrine of revelation in the Old Testament. Its message is that God makes himself known through his creation of the universe (verses 1–6); through his law (verses 7–10); and through his relationship with each individual (verses 11–14). People under pressure who can comprehend these revelations will be well on the path towards finding a God-centred way of solving their problems.

The author of this psalm was an artist of genius. His first six verses unveil a panorama of pictures and ideas which illuminate the handiwork of God our creator. He reveals his glory in the majesty and mystery of the night sky and in the warmth and splendour of the daytime. Using the terrestrial image of continuous continuity *day after day... night after night* and the celestial paradox of inaudible audibility: *There is neither speech nor language where their voice is not heard* (verses 2–3), we are taken from the heights of the heavens (verse 1) to the end of the world (verse 4) in a mere 55 words of exquisite poetry.

In the next two verses the psalmist exercises some artistic humour at the expense of sun god worshippers, believers in astrology and their ilk. Far from elevating the sun to the be-all and end-all of the universe we are told that God has merely *pitched a tent for the sun* (verse 5) somewhere in his heavens. At first the sun is portrayed as a bridegroom emerging from his tent on his wedding day. Then changing from the analogy of the bridegroom to that of a champion athlete the sun runs a circuit across the heavens. *Nothing is hidden from its heat* (verse 6) adds the author.

That last line is the link line to the next section of the psalm (verses 7–11) which tells us that God reveals himself in his law. The connection here is that the sun's rays are all cleansing, all detecting, all purifying. So is God's law, known in ancient Israel as Torah, and laid down in Old Testament scripture. From the five nouns and accompanying adjectives used by the psalmist to describe the law several surprising ideas emerge. Those who have been involved in modern litigation may have some difficulty in accepting the notion that the law can revive the soul, give joy to the heart, bring light to the eyes and taste sweeter than honey. But what the psalmist was conveying was that the Torah was not just a set of rules governing human behaviour. God's law as revealed in scripture was his way of making himself known to his people.

The final part of the psalm (verses 11–14) explains how God becomes known to the individual. The author has moved from the macro revelation of God and the universe to the micro relationship between God and himself. He has obeyed the warnings of the law and derived from his rightness with God the *great reward* (verse 11) of inner peace. He asks to be delivered from major and minor sins. In the final verse, much used by preachers before they begin their sermons, the psalmist prays that his words and thoughts will always please his Lord, his Rock and his Redeemer.

C. S. Lewis wrote of Psalm 19: 'I take this to be the greatest poem in the Psalter and one of the greatest lyrics in the world' (34). Many would agree with him. The combination of beautiful imagery with profound theology has inspired writers and composers down the ages and has influenced the spirituality of untold millions. The message our pressurised contemporary world can take from the psalm is that God is to be found in the beauty of nature, in the keeping of his laws, and in the building of a personal relationship with him.

ADDITIONAL NOTES

Form and Title: This is a wisdom psalm ending in a personal prayer. Much academic ink has been spilt on the question of whether it was originally written as two psalms. C. S. Lewis seems to have been the first major dissenter from the hybrid psalm consensus of most scholars. Perhaps it took a 20th century poet to identify the 1000 BC poet's linkage in verse 6 between the cleansing power of God's sun and God's law (see Reflection). There are no hiding places from either.

Of David: Because there is no historical setting for this timeless psalm in the annals of David's life, there are no grounds for attributing the authorship to him personally.

Verses 7–11: The five nouns are used frequently as synonyms for law throughout Psalm 19. The five adjectives are capable of multiple interpretations as are the five verbs. This is a rich passage for personal meditation as well as scholarly opinion.

Verse 12: *Who can discern his errors?* C. H. Spurgeon suggests that this sentence should end with an exclamation mark rather than a question mark, arguing that as a question it provides its own answer. For it is not clear what the psalmist thought were his undiscernible *hidden sins*. Had he forgotten them, committed them unwittingly or in ignorance? Most sins are *wilful* (Verse 13).

Verse 13: *The great transgression*: This divides many preachers and commentators; e.g., John Bunyan thought it was blasphemy, Dick Lucas, idolatry, C. S. Lewis, pride. Under Mosaic law it probably meant adultery. John Stott says it does not refer to any one particularly grievous sin but to all deliberate wrongdoing committed 'defiantly' (see Numbers 15: 30–31) (35).

Verses 14–15: This prayer was for centuries almost as frequently used in Christian worship as the apostolic benediction.

PERSONAL COMMENT

One of my favourite pieces of choral music is Haydn's exultant anthem 'The heavens are telling the glory of God'. One of my favourite hymns is Joseph Addison's 'The spacious firmament on high' which has the sun, moon and stars 'for ever singing as they shine: The hand that made us is divine' (36).

I must have sung both of them many times from my school choirboy days onwards. But it took a few months in a prison cell before I discovered what they meant and who was their original source of inspiration – the author of Psalm 19.

The outward manifestations of creation's glory have stirred human imaginations towards an understanding of God since time immemorial. I came across a good 20th century example of this phenomenon recently when writing the biography of Charles W. Colson, the founder of Prison Fellowship who is today America's best known Christian leader after Billy Graham.

In 1959 Colson was a 2nd Lieutenant in the US Marines sailing towards the coast of Guatemala under orders to invade that small South American country. Like all the other young men on board the ships of the task force, he was nervous at the prospect of making an amphibious landing on beaches defended by Communist rebels. At that time Colson was such an unchurched and Godless 18-year-old that he did not know even the most familiar of Bible stories such as the Good Samaritan or the Prodigal Son. Yet one evening he went up on deck as his warship, the *USS Mellette*, steamed towards Guatemala and gazed in awe and wonder at the starry sky above him. 'That night I suddenly became as certain as I had ever been about anything in my life that out there in that starlit beyond was God', wrote Colson in his autobiography *Born Again*. 'I was convinced that He ruled over the universe, that to Him there were no mysteries, that somehow He kept it miraculously in order. In my own fumbling way, I prayed, knowing that He was there ...' (43).

Colson's teenage prayers did not take him far on his spiritual journey at that time. Even though the heavens had declared the glory of God to him, he spent the next two and a half decades of his life rejecting and disobeying God's law. Like me, Colson was such an arrogant, high-flying, and eventually law-breaking polit-ical figure that he had to be humbled by a prison sentence before he got his relationship with God right.

As this psalm makes clear, acknowledging the power of God the creator and surrendering our will to the authority of god the law-giver are the vital steps we have to take before God reveals himself to us.

A PRAYER BASED ON PSALM 19

O Lord you have revealed yourself to me in glory of your creation, from the hot sunshine of the day to the starry beauty of the night.

You have also revealed yourself to me in the power of your word, your teachings, and your commandments.

Lord, help me to stay faithful to your laws. Keep me from my wilful sins. Cleanse me from my secret faults.

May the words of my mouth and the thoughts of my heart be always acceptable in your sight, O Lord my Rock and my Redeemer. Amen.

PSALM 46: God in catastrophe

For the director of music. Of the Sons of Korah.
According to alamoth. A song.

God is our refuge and strength,
  an ever-present help in trouble.
[2] Therefore we will not fear, though the earth give way
  and the mountains fall into the heart of the sea,
[3] though its waters roar and foam
  and the mountains quake with their surging.
Selah

[4] There is a river whose streams make glad the city of God,
  the holy place where the Most High dwells.
[5] God is within her, she will not fall;
  God will help her at break of day.
[6] Nations are in uproar, kingdoms fall;
  he lifts his voice, the earth melts.

[7] The Lord Almighty is with us;
  the God of Jacob is our fortress.
Selah

[8] Come and see the works of the Lord,
  the desolations he has brought on the earth.
[9] He makes wars cease to the ends of the earth;
  he breaks the bow and shatters the spear,
  he burns the shields with fire.
[10] 'Be still, and know that I am God;
  I will be exalted among the nations,
  I will be exalted in the earth.'

[11] The Lord Almighty is with us;
  the God of Jacob is our fortress.
Selah

REFLECTION

God offers the only confident assurance of help and strength in a catastrophe-prone world. This mighty psalm, which has given comfort down the ages as a hymn of impregnability, will reach out with a powerful message to people under pressure from the 21st century's vulnerability to man-made and natural disasters.

The psalm divides into three parts, each characterised by a different literary tone and separated by the musical direction word *Selah* which is thought to mean a change of voices.

The first part (verses 1–3) is a defiant declaration of confidence. Not only is God our refuge and strength. We will not be afraid even if we have to face earthquakes, explosions, floods and mountains falling into the sea. Saying that we should believe this is faith at its most romantic. Believing it when we are caught in the middle of a 9/11, an earthquake or a flood is faith at its most challenging. The ancient people of Israel rose to the challenge because of their experiences.

The second part of the psalm (verses 4–7) describes an experience of deliverance from catastrophe. The tone of the author's poetry undergoes a surprising change. The waters that were roaring and foaming in verse 3 become the gentle streams of a life-giving river that symbolises God's grace. It gladdens the holy city where He dwells (verse 4). This is Zion which will never fall even when nations are in uproar and melting away (verses 5–6).

In the third part of the psalm the author praises God for his protection and for destroying Israel's enemies and their military equipment. This is probably an historical reference to some epic deliverance of Jerusalem from one of the sieges by attacking armies it faced during the first millennia BC. The destruction of Sennacherib's Assyrian army in 701 BC by plague when it was encamped outside the walls of Jerusalem is the most likely episode to have been in the psalmist's mind.

The most dramatic moment in this triumphant account of past deliverances comes when God intervenes with the words: *Be still and know that I am God* (verse 10). It is an instruction that people under pressure, so often subsumed in the noise, hustle and bustle of their worldly priorities, would do well to take to heart. Sometimes it takes a crisis or a catastrophe to bring us unto contact with God. But if we want to listen to him and get to know him we must follow his command: *Be still.*

'Nothing in all creation is so like God as stillness' wrote the 14th century German mystic Meister Eckhart (38). When we commune with our creator in stillness we begin to see why he should be *exalted among the nations ... exalted in the earth* (verse 5). For our only security, and our only secure route to his heavenly city of Zion, lies in putting our trust in Him.

ADDITIONAL NOTES

Form and Title: This is a hymn of confidence, intended to be sung by a congregation in liturgical form, with other voices intervening. The title confirms its musical significance.

According to Alamoth: Means treble voices.

Sons of Korah: See note to Psalm 42. It is widely believed that the psalm was composed at a time of great crisis with direct references to the historical episode of the deliverance of Jerusalem in 701 BC (see Reflection).

Verse 2: *the mountains fall into the sea*: In the ancient world the mountains symbolised the pillars of the earth holding it in place over the waters (see Job 9: 5–6).

Verse 4: *A river whose streams make glad the city of God*: This may refer to the waters of Siloam whose gentle flow was portrayed by Isaiah as symbolising the quiet, beneficial providence of God (Isaiah 8: 6). The city itself was Zion, where God dwells. Some psalms picture it as a heavenly rather than earthly location (see Psalm 48).

Verse 6: *Nations are in uproar, kingdoms fall ... the earth melts*: The psalmist is presenting 'cosmic collapse and the chaos of political upheaval as parallel forces' (39).

Lifts his voice: Is an allusion to God's thunder (see Psalms 18: 13, 68: 33, 77: 17).

Verse 11: *The Lord Almighty is with us*: This majestic affirmation has echoes of Isaiah's great prophecy on Immanuel: 'God is with us' (Isaiah 7: 14, 8: 8, 8: 10).

Psalm as a whole: 'The name of Martin Luther will always be associated with this psalm. His famous hymn "Ein' feste Burg ist unser Gott" is a free paraphrase of it. He and Philip Melancthon would sing it together in times of dark discouragement and Thomas Carlyle has made it familiar to English readers by his translation "A Safe Stronghold our God is still". It is a sublime expression of quiet confidence in God's sovereignty amid the upheavals of nature and history' (40).

PERSONAL COMMENT

One of the most influential guides on my spiritual journey has been a short book *Be still and know ...* by Michael Ramsey, Archbishop of Canterbury 1961–1974. From a starting point of stillness with God it suggests well-tried routes of prayer in areas of spirituality such as contemplative meditation. It is a gem of holy wisdom from a great Christian leader and theologian.

For most of the first 57 years of my life I was too busy with the pressures and temptations of the world to follow the key advice of Michael Ramsey's book and of this psalm: *Be still and know that I am God* (verse 10). Then I was hit by catastrophe and went to prison.

Like many a monk in past centuries I discovered that a cell can be a good place to pray in. Like many an early rising prisoner I discovered that a sleeping jail can be majestic in its stillness between the hours of an early summer dawn and the raucous shouts of 'Unlock! Everybody out!' with which officers rouse inmates at 7.30 am. So it was during those hours that I first discovered how to be still before the Lord, how to listen to him, be in awe of him, and get to know him.

Does it take a personal or national catastrophe to shock the restless soul into seeking stillness with God? It need not. There are many better and easier paths to divine understanding. Yet it is true that times of disaster can be harbingers of a quiet new start to the way we begin listening to God.

One of my favourite passages in the Old Testament is the story of Elijah fleeing to Mount Horeb after slaughtering the prophets of Baal (1 Kings 19: 1–18). Elijah has fled for his life. He is exhausted in body and broken in spirit. He wants to die. But the Lord has other plans. So Elijah is woken up in his cave on Mount Horeb, first by a mighty rushing wind, then by an earthquake and then by a fire. The Lord is not in any of them. But then there comes a gentle whisper (NIV) or a still small voice (King James Bible). It is the voice of God which Elijah hears perfectly in the stillness after the earthquake wind and fire, and which gives him commands that renew his life and ministry.

God's mysterious purposes can be communicated to us in mysterious ways. Tragedies, disasters and catastrophes may seem the most unbearable and unbelievable signals of a new and God-guided purpose in our lives. Are we willing to listen to those signals, to decode them and to act upon them? There is only one way to start the process. It is to *Be still and know that I am God* (verse 10).

A PRAYER BASED ON PSALM 46

O Lord God, you are our refuge and strength, an ever present help in trouble.

Help us not to be afraid when we are caught in a crisis or a catastrophe. Give us the strength to see that your life-giving streams of love flow through even the worst of disasters and will sustain us.

In the worst of our troubles help us to heed the wisdom of this psalm and to obey its command: *Be still and know that I am God*. In the stillness we offer you, may we hear your voice and know your will, through Jesus Christ Our Lord. Amen.

PSALM 48: God as our guide

A song. A psalm of the Sons of Korah.

Great is the Lord, and most worthy of praise,
    in the city of our God, his holy mountain.
[2] It is beautiful in its loftiness,
    the joy of the whole earth.
Like the utmost heights of Zaphon is Mount Zion,
    the city of the Great King.
[3] God is in her citadels;
    he has shown himself to be her fortress.

[4] When the kings joined forces,
    when they advanced together,
[5] they saw {her} and were astounded;
    they fled in terror.
[6] Trembling seized them there,
    pain like that of a woman in labour.
[7] You destroyed them like ships of Tarshish
    shattered by an east wind.

[8] As we have heard,
so have we seen
in the city of the Lord Almighty,
in the city of our God:
God makes her secure for ever.
Selah

[9] Within your temple, O God,
    we meditate on your unfailing love.
[10] Like your name, O God,
    your praise reaches to the ends of the earth;
    your right hand is filled with righteousness.
[11] Mount Zion rejoices,
    the villages of Judah are glad
    because of your judgments.

[12] Walk about Zion, go round her,
    count her towers,

[13] consider well her ramparts,
   view her citadels,
   that you may tell of them to the next generation.
[14] For this God is our God for ever and ever;
   he will be our guide even to the end.

REFLECTION

There are many ways of reaching out to God. This psalm suggests we should praise him in his heavenly abode. For worldly centres of power are insecure and crumble under pressure. Only God will stay with us as our everlasting guide.

The psalm opens on a swelling note of praise. As Kidner notes: 'There is much in common here with Psalm 46, not least with its atmosphere of elation after a great deliverance' (41) (Kidner, p. 179). We are inside God's holy city and the view is *beautiful in its loftiness, the joy of the whole earth* (verse 2). The sweep of this panorama, and the fact that the city's time horizons are also without limits (verse 14) suggests that we are in a heavenly place.

The heavenly city of Zion is on a mountain lower than some of the neighbouring peaks like Zaphon (verse 2). The psalmist is subtly making the theological point that God does not choose the highest and strongest places (or people) to come and dwell in. However, when God does take up residence, he creates a fortress of total invincibility. If alien visitors advance towards it they are astounded. Kings flee; strong men tremble like women in the pains of childbirth; mighty ships are shattered in the wind (verses 4–7). This is a poetic way of saying that man's power offers no security whereas God's power gives absolute security.

The worshippers of Israel understood all this. In the temple they meditate on God's unfailing love. In the villages of Judah they are rejoicing. In the last three verses we see a procession of faithful praise-givers marching round the towers, ramparts and citadels of Zion so that they can see them and pass on a message to succeeding generations (verses 12–14).

That message is a strong one, particularly to people under pressure from the powers and winds of worldly fortune referred to in verses 4–7. As Zion's people know such forces are illusory and transient. The walk of worshippers around those symbolic towers and ramparts is a way of strengthening faith in the intangible but greater reality of the God who will be *our God for ever and ever* and *our guide even to the end* (verse 14).

ADDITIONAL NOTES

Form and title: This is one of six Zion psalms (the others are 46, 76, 87, 125, 129), so called because they emphasise that God dwells in this holy city. Jesus quoted verse 2 to make this same point in the sermon on the mount (Matthew 5: 35). The psalmist combines the ideas of the earthly Zion (Jerusalem) with the heavenly one.

It is clear from the double title, *A Song. A Psalm,* that this was a popular musical event. Verse 10 suggests that it was part of temple liturgy and verse 13 implies that this may have been part of a wider liturgy that involved a procession around the city.

Sons of Korah: See note to Psalm 42.

Verse 2: *Heights of Zaphon*: A specific mountain North of Ugarit in modern-day Syria. It was higher than Zion and sacred to Baal worshippers.

Verse 4: *Kings*: Some translations render this as 'Kings of the earth'.

Verse 7: *ships of Tarshish*: Huge ocean-going ships built by the Phoenicians. They were regarded as symbols of maritime power.

Verse 11: *villages of Judah*: In some translations are daughters of Judah.

Psalm as a whole: In some Christian traditions Psalm 48 was the appointed Psalm for Whitsunday or Pentecost because Jerusalem (synonymous with Zion) was the birthplace of the early church.

PERSONAL COMMENT

Many years ago I was a spectator at a ceremony known as 'beating the bounds' in the City of Canterbury. All I can remember about it is that a choir processed round the walls of the old city singing hymns and psalms. As we reached various landmarks, along the medieval wall of the city, a choirboy was 'beaten' (in fact tapped symbolically on his shoulder with a piece of bamboo) so that he and the crowd would remember the boundary lines between those parishes which were within or without the ancient city.

At the time it seemed a meaningless, if colourful, piece of ecclesiastical ritual whose purpose had long ago been lost in the mists of time. I would guess that the ceremonies described in verses 12–13 of Psalm 48 were not so very different. For it seems that singers and musicians led by the sons of Korah may have processed round the fortifications of ancient Jerusalem singing praises to God their guide and protector. Did this cultic ritual have any point to it? Yes, to glorify at the strongholds of power in the city's physical defences the more intangible but far greater power of God. Worship, in whatever the appropriate form of the age may be, is man's way of honouring the King of heaven with thanks and praise.

A PRAYER BASED ON PSALM 48

O God, Great King of Zion, ruler of the universe and Lord of all human hearts we come to give you thanks and praise. All earthly power is nothing in comparison to your power. Help us to understand this and to rejoice in your eternal greatness. As we travel on our journey towards you and your heavenly city may we pass on to succeeding generations the knowledge that you are our God for ever and ever and that you will be our guide even to the end. Amen.

PSALM 87: God of surprises

Of the Sons of Korah. A psalm. A song.

He has set his foundation on the holy mountain;
    [2] the Lord loves the gates of Zion
    more than all the dwellings of Jacob.
[3] Glorious things are said of you,
    O city of God:
Selah

[4] 'I will record Rahab and Babylon
    among those who acknowledge me –
Philistia too, and Tyre, along with Cush –
    and will say, "This one was born in Zion."'

[5] Indeed, of Zion it will be said,
    'This one and that one were born in her,
    and the Most High himself will establish her.'
[6] The Lord will write in the register of the peoples:
    'This one was born in Zion.'
Selah

[7] As they make music they will sing,
    'All my fountains are in you.'

REFLECTION

This short psalm has an important message for some types of people who feel under pressure. It is: God loves outsiders, former enemies, and the excluded. He longs to welcome them into his heavenly home, and to pour his grace on them. He is the inclusive God of all people.

Because the language and the names in this psalm are rather obscure, it is easy to miss their significance and the historical background to them. This psalm was written at least five centuries before the coming of Christ. At that time the people of Israel believed themselves to be God's chosen people. Their religion was exclusive. Only a faithful follower of it could possibly gain entry to Zion, the holy and heavenly mountain where God dwells.

These views are reflected throughout the psalter and particularly in five of the six Zion psalms (46, 48, 76, 125, 129) which describe God's dwelling place. According to them, Zion might just as well have had a notice on its gates saying 'No admission except to the people of Israel'.

Psalm 87 is a Zion psalm with a difference. It overturned conventional Israelite wisdom in its approach. For by the end of its seven verses there can be no doubt of its message that the nations Israel hated, fought against and shunned would one day be loved and welcomed by God as fellow citizens of heaven.

The psalm opens with a typical paean of praise (verses 1–3). God founded Zion and loves it. So does the author. His line about the glorious things said of the heavenly city inspired John Newton's great hymn: 'Glorious things of thee are spoken, Zion City of our God' (42).

In verse 4 God starts speaking. He declares he will record in his register of Zion-born inhabitants five groups of future believers who had hitherto been Israel's enemies. Rahab means the loathed Egyptians from whom the Israelites escaped in the Exodus. Babylon means the hated powers of Mesopotamia who took the Israelites into exile. Philistia means the feared Philistines who were Israel's traditional enemies on the battlefield. Tyre means the envied merchants and traders of neighbouring Phoenicia. Cush is a generic term for distant far away nations such as the peoples of Ethiopia, Sudan and other parts of Africa.

The idea that people from these heathen nations could join God's chosen people of Israel as equals in Zion was revolutionary. Yet God was saying that *those who acknowledge me* (verse 4) would be granted full native-born status in his holy city. Acknowledging the Lord meant knowing him personally, a relationship believed to be the exclusive privilege of the Israelites. God was thinking on a much bigger scale.

It is not until the time of the New Testament that the scope of God's vision was made plain. *Go and make disciples of all nations* (Matthew 28: 19) was Jesus Christ's final command to his followers. In the early church this came to mean the baptising of both Jews and Gentiles. We now know that God welcomes anyone of any race, nation, or social class, no matter how much they were previously under pressure as sinners or outcasts, if they acknowledge him. As in ancient Israel, this means having a faithful relationship with God and accepting the gift of his grace. A second spiritual citizenship is granted to those who are born again in this way in Zion – which is rightly presented in this psalm as a community of believers rather than as a geographical location.

Finally the born again citizens of Zion get one more blessing mentioned in the last verse of this psalm. The line *all my fountains are in you* (verse 7) is difficult to translate from the Hebrew. Other versions of the Bible speak of rivers, springs, and waters overflowing. What the psalmist was saying is that Zion is not only a city of glory, open to all believers. It is also a place of spiritual refreshment whose inhabitants are constantly watered by the fountains of God's grace. People under pressure should start thinking about how to get there, as no-one need be excluded from this heavenly community.

ADDITIONAL NOTES

Form and Title: This is a Zion psalm (see note to Psalm 48 for further details), but it stands in lonely isolation in the psalter because of its revolutionary thinking towards Israel's enemies (see Reflection).

Of the Sons of Korah: See note to Psalm 42 on pages 25–26.

A psalm. A song: These two terms are difficult to define. The first was a carefully composed formal poem usually accompanied by musical instruments. The second was a more popular and widely sung poem. The double title may suggest that it was performed in both settings.

Verse 2: *Dwellings of Jacob*: A synonym for Israel.

Verse 3: *Selah*: See note to Psalm 4 on page 76.

Verse 4: *Rahab*, etc: See Reflection.

Verse 5: *born in her*: The birth image here evokes several passages in Israel in which Zion is depicted as a mother surprised by the number of her children (see Isaiah 49: 20–21; 54: 1; 66: 7–8). St Paul also utilises the mother role of Zion: 'The Jerusalem above ... she is our mother', he wrote in Galatians 4: 26.

Verse 6: *The register of the peoples*: See Malachi 3: 16 ('a scroll of remembrance was written in his presence concerning those who feared the Lord') and Revelation 21: 27 ('the book of life').

Verse 7: *All my fountains*: See Reflection.

Psalm as a whole: The vision of Psalm 87 was fulfilled by the work of St Paul, the apostle to the Gentiles. 'This grace was given to me to preach to the Gentiles the unsearchable riches of Christ and to make plain to everyone the administration of this mystery which for ages past was kept hidden in God', he wrote in Ephesians 3: 8–9.

PERSONAL COMMENT

While I was reading theology at Oxford, I was set an essay with the interesting title 'What is heaven and who will get into it?' Although I duly spread myself across several thousand words of typescript I concluded that the answer boiled down to this:

Heaven is where God dwells and its population will be full of surprises.

Psalm 87 must have surprised the Israelites who thought they alone were God's chosen people. But all pious people have to learn that the righteous are not a self-appointing sect. God's grace cannot be deserved or earned. It is His gift.

Soon after I began reading the psalms regularly I met someone who I felt sure had received this gift. God's grace shone through him. He was a prisoner. In his past he had displayed the worst qualities of the ancient Babylonians, Philistines and Egyptians put together. He was as black as the far away people of Cush. But he had been transformed by his experiences of 'acknowledging' God and all that flows from it. He had so obviously been saved by grace through faith that his admission to the City of God seems to me to be a certainty. His kindness and goodness to the least and worst of his fellow prisoners flowed so generously that the final line of this psalm, *All my fountains are in you*, could have been written for him. God is full of surprises, not least towards the excluded.

A PRAYER BASED ON PSALM 87

Heavenly Father, thank you for being the God of surprises who excludes no-one from your Kingdom and includes the most improbable people. We thank you for the peoples mentioned in this psalm who turned to you in faith and were welcomed into your holy city. We pray that we may follow in their footsteps, and sing of your glory as we are refreshed by the heavenly fountains of your grace. Through Jesus Christ our Lord. Amen.

PSALM 146: Praise the Lord

Praise the Lord.

Praise the Lord, O my soul.
[2] I will praise the Lord all my life;
I will sing praise to my God as long as I live.

[3] Do not put your trust in princes,
in mortal men, who cannot save.
[4] When their spirit departs, they return to the ground;
on that very day their plans come to nothing.

[5] Blessed is he whose help is the God of Jacob,
whose hope is in the Lord his God,
[6] the Maker of heaven and earth,
the sea, and everything in them –
the Lord, who remains faithful for ever.
[7] He upholds the cause of the oppressed
and gives food to the hungry.
The Lord sets prisoners free,
[8] the Lord gives sight to the blind,
the Lord lifts up those who are bowed down,
the Lord loves the righteous.
[9] The Lord watches over the alien
and sustains the fatherless and the widow,
but he frustrates the ways of the wicked.

[10] The Lord reigns for ever,
your God, O Zion, for all generations.

Praise the Lord.

REFLECTION

It seems right to end this little book on the psalms with the same note of thanks and praise as the psalter itself ends on. The last five psalms in the bible are known as the Hallelujah psalms because they all open and close with the words *Praise the Lord*, a literal translation of the Hebrew words Hallelū (O Praise) Jāh (the Lord or Yahweh). This psalm not only praises God but describes him in the final verses by telling of nine categories of people under pressure whom the Lord loves and protects.

After the exultant shout of *Praise the Lord*, the psalmist gives a warning about human mortality. *Do not put your trust in princes* (verse 2) may seem an archaic admonition to a modern world in which few princes exist. But Kidner, as usual, hits the nail on the head by suggesting that a contemporary translation of princes should be 'influential people' (43). For as the psalmist implies in verses 3–4, today's celebrities, movers and shakers, power brokers and billionaires are all going the way of yesterday's princes; *to the ground* where *their plans come to nothing* (verse 4). The same thought was expressed by William Shakespeare in one of his most beautiful verses:

'Golden lads and girls all must,
As chimney sweepers come to dust' (44).

The next verse of the psalm defines the blessed person who is heading for a higher destination, God's heavenly abode of Zion (verse 10). It is the person who has hoped in and been helped by the Lord (verse 5).

This Lord is faithful to people under pressure who believe in him. Nine categories of them are mentioned by the psalmist whose list could not have been intended to be exhaustive. Even so it is intriguing and far reaching. It includes *the oppressed, the hungry, prisoners, the blind, the bowed down, the righteous, the alien, the fatherless, and the widow* (verses 7–9). If the broadest definitions are applied to these groups, the scope of God's blessings becomes huge. For example, if the hungry means the spiritually hungry; prisoners means prisoners of sin; the righteous means those whose good lives have not brought them good earthly rewards; the alien means the alienated; or the fatherless means those who have missed out on right relationships with their earthly or heavenly father, then the Lord's help is vast in its range.

The one group of people whom the Lord is not going to help are the wicked (verse 12). Judgement awaits them. After this sombre warning the psalm reminds us that the God of heaven is a God of eternity, so *Praise the Lord* (verse 10).

ADDITIONAL NOTES

Form and Title: No title here but possibly because the last five psalms are all covered by the title of Psalm 145, *A psalm of praise*.

Verse 5: *God of Jacob*: Means in this context the God of all faithful believers. It may also be the psalmist's subtle reminder that Jacob was hungry, thirsty and under pressure when God befriended him. In this psalm as in Psalm 46: 7–11 (see page 125) the God of Jacob is associated with help and protection.

Verse 9: *frustrates the way of the wicked*: This is a mealy-mouthed translation. Much better is Coverdale's 'the way of the wicked he turneth it upside down'. They are going to get their come-uppance.

PERSONAL COMMENT

As a schoolboy I recall being spellbound by a teacher enacting the last words on the scaffold of Thomas Wentworth, Earl of Strafford. King Charles I had promised Strafford that he should never suffer in 'life, honour or fortune'. But political pressure changed the King's mind and Charles signed the Royal Assent for the Act of Attainder. As Strafford went to his execution as a result of this terrible act of royal betrayal he quoted Psalm 146, verse 3, in the old fashioned language of his time: 'Put not your trust in princes nor in the sons of men for in them there is no salvation' (45).

Princes are all about principalities or the prizes of this world. In this psalm they symbolise 'the wicked' which is a harsh piece of poetic licence by the author for princes have souls like all the rest of us, sometimes good and righteous souls. It is the quality of our spiritual souls not the quality of our worldly power and possessions which will be scrutinised by God at the time of our judgement. So we must trust in him alone for salvation.

This psalm increases our understanding of God because it tells us who and what he cares most about. The nine figurative categories of people under pressure (verses 7–9) are encouraging. A God who loves those of us who fall into one or more of these groups deserves our adoration. That is one of the reasons why I have written this book and why I end it with the same words as the author ended this and each one of the last five psalms in the psalter: *Praise the Lord.*

A PRAYER BASED ON PSALM 146

Praise the Lord, O my soul, Praise the Lord! For you are our hope and strength. We trust in you, not in the influential and important people of the world. You love your children who come under pressure. Thank you for caring for the oppressed, the hungry, the prisoners, the blind, the bowed down, the righteous, the alien, the fatherless and the widows. You are the King of heaven and the God of eternity. Praise the Lord, O my soul, Praise the Lord! Amen.

BIBLIOGRAPHY

Anderson, A. A. (1972) *Psalms* (2 vols) (London, NCB Oliphants).

Anderson, B. W. (1983) *Out of the Depths* (Philadelphia, Westminster Press).

Allen, Leslie (1986) *Psalms 101–150* (Waco, Texas, Word Books).

Briggs, C. A., & Briggs, E. G. (1906) *A Critical and Exegetical Commentary on the Book of the Psalms* (Edinburgh, T. & T. Clark).

Broyles, Craig C. (1999) *Psalms* (Peabody, Massachusetts, Hendrickson Publishers).

Brueggemann, W. (1984) *The Message of the Psalms* (Minneapolis, Augsburg, Augsburg Old Testament Studies).

Calvin, John (1845) *Commentary on the Book of Psalms* (3 vols) (Edinburgh).

Clements, Roy (1993) *Songs of Experience* (Fearn, Ross-shire, Christian Focus Publications).

Coggan, Donald (1998) *Psalms 1–72 and 73–150* (2 vols) (Oxford, The Bible Reading Fellowship).

Craigie, Peter C. (1986) *Psalms 1–150* (Waco, Texas, Word Books).

Eaton, J. H. (1967) *Psalms* (London, SCM Press).

Gunkel, H. (1926) *Die Psalmen* (Gottingen).

Keil, C. F. and Delitzsch, H. (1984) *Psalms* (Grand Rapids, Michigan, Erdmans).

Kidner, Derek (1973–1975) *Psalms 1–72 and 73–150* (2 vols) (London, IVP).

Kirkpatrick, A. F. (1902) *The Book of Psalms* (Cambridge, CUP).

Kraus, H.-J. (1988–1989) *Psalms. A Commentary* (2 vols), Translated by H. C. Oswald (Augsburg, Minneapolis).

Lewis, C. S. (1961) *Reflections on the Psalms* (London, Harper Collins).

Longman, Tremper, (1983) *How to Read the Psalms* (Leicester, IVP).

Lloyd-Jones, Martyn (1965) *Faith on Trial: Studies in Psalm 73* (London, IVP).

Mowinckel, S. G. (1962) *The Psalms in Israel's Worship* (2 vols) (Oxford, Blackwell).

Perowne, J. J. S. (1976) *The Book of Psalms* (Michigan, Grand Rapids, Zondervan).

Rogerson, J. W. and Mackay, J. W. (1977) *Psalms 1–50; 51–100; 100–150* (3 vols) (Cambridge, Cambridge Bible Commentary, CUP).

Spurgeon, C. H. (1989) *The Treasury of David* (3 vols) (Peabody, Massachusetts, Hendrickson Publishers).

Stott, John, *Favourite Psalms* (Milton Keynes, Word UK).

Tate, M. E. (1990) *Psalms 51–100* (Dallas, Word Books).

Wilcock, Michael (2001) *The Message of the Psalms 1–72 and 73–150* (2 vols) (Leicester, IVP).

SOURCES

1. Augustine Psalms, Folio XXI, p. 320. See also Spurgeon, p. 574.
2. Stott, p. 124.
3. Kidner, p. 332.
4. William Shakespeare, *Midsummer Night's Dream*, Act 2, Scene 4.
5. Anecdote told to the author by E. W. Swanton.
6. Lloyd Jones, *Spiritual Depression*, p. 82.
7. *Salad Days*, Julian Slade, Act 2, and Reprise.
8. Conversation between the author and Canon Michael Green, The Radcliffe Infirmary, Oxford, 21 November 2001.
9. B. W. Anderson, p. 42.
10. Kidner, p. 262.
11. Wilcock, p. 260.
12. Luther, *Table Talk*, p. 171.
13. Spurgeon, p. 249.
14. Wilcock, p. 78.
15. Kidner, p. 107.
16. Mowinckel, *Psalmstudien*, p. 41.
17. For a longer account of my relationship with Sister Mary Finbar, see my book *Pride and Perjury* (Continuum, 2003), pp. 93–101.
18. Henry Fielding, *Tom Jones*, p. 103.
19. Kidner, p. 88.
20. Spurgeon, p. 215.
21. Broyles, p. 101.
22. C. W. Colson, letter to the author, 14 October 1997.
23. Kidner, p. 435.
24. Kidner, p. 306.
25. Stott, p. 74.
26. Luther, *Table Talk*, p. 389.
27. William Shakespeare, *Hamlet*, Act 3, Scene 2.
28. Article by the author, *Spectator*, 18 December 1997.
29. Augustine, *Psalms*, Folio XIV, p. 27.
30. William Temple, *Psalm Sunday to Easter* (SPCK), p. 88.
31. Kidner, p. 121.
32. *Evening Standard*, 12 April 2000.
33. Stott, p. 52.
34. Lewis, p. 56.
35. Stott, p. 23.
36. Joseph Addison, Hymn 'The Spacious Firmament on High'.
37. C. W. Colson, *Born Again*, p. 26.
38. Meister Eikhart, *c.* 1260–1327/8.
39. Broyles, p. 210.
40. Stott, p. 58.
41. Kidner, p. 179.

42. John Newton, Hymn 'Glorious things of thee are spoken'.
43. Kidner, p. 483.
44. William Shakespeare, 'Fear no more the heat o' the sun'.
45. Strafford, *Veronica Wedgwood*, p. 317.